CREATING THE "A" TEAM

*A Motivational Guide
For Multi-Line Insurance Agents
And Small Business Owners*

To my parents Carmen and Al Sicard Sr.,

who sacrificed so much and prepared me so well

for such incredible opportunities

To Janelle,

who shared more than a decade with me on this joyful adventure,

you have my eternal gratitude

To Mari,

who made me better physically, mentally and spiritually

CREATING THE "A" TEAM

A Motivational Guide
For Multi-Line Insurance Agents
And Small Business Owners

by

Al Sicard

Copyright © 2010 by Al Sicard

All rights reserved.

No part of this book may be used in whole or in part, or reproduced in any manner whatsoever, without written permission of the author.

For information about obtaining additional copies of this book or for permission to reproduce selections from this book, please contact:

AL Sicard
1336 Woodman Drive
Dayton, Ohio 45432-3496

Phone: (937) 256-1806
Toll Free: (888) 667-6536
Fax: (937) 256-2802

This book is printed on acid-free paper
First edition, 2010
Manufactured in the United States of America

Creating the "A" Team
ISBN 978-0-615-35609-9

Contents

About this Book	viii
Introduction	ix

Part I

Creating the "A" Team	1
Owning Your Own Business	5
New Agent Graveyard	7
Systems to Create an Organization That Works Without You	22
For All Systems: I Don't Care What Way We Do It, But That We Do It the Same Way	25
AL Sicard's System	27
Chart: How Most Insurance Agencies Are Organized	30
Chart: How AL's System is Organized	31
Leads	32
Graphic: AL's Marketing Funnel	33
Retention and Referrals	35
Lead Conversion	36

The 2-Minute Drill	37
If You See It or Hear It, Record It	41
Impressions	43
Scoreboard	44
The Quote	48
Selling	52
Baby Terms	53
Complaints: Focus on the Important Few	55
McDonald's Consistency and Routines	58
Office Decorum	59
Team Meetings	61
Perfect Day	63
Stress Buster	68
Advisory Boards: Mentors, Teachers & Coaches	70
Award vs. Reward	74
Newsletters	76
Branding	78
Fire Someone	79

Part II

Creating the "A" Team Agency Draft	83
The Tryouts	86

Welcome Packet	90
Motivation	91
Training	93
Flight School	97
Community Service	101
Implementing AL's System	104
Implementing AL's Systems: a Neighborly Approach	110
On Date Night Don't Forget Your Family	117

Part III

Player Haters	119
Your Company's Management	121

Part IV

Stories of Success	125
Speedy	171
Summary	179
BigAlf.com	182
About the Author	183

About This Book

The opinions and the information provided are those of the author and are not endorsed, nor approved for use by State Farm Mutual Automobile Insurance Company, nor by its affiliates, subsidiaries, agents, agent's staff, or employees. State Farm Mutual Automobile Insurance Company, its affiliates, subsidiaries, agents or agent's staff make no representations as to the accuracy of the statements and/or content of this material.

State Farm Agents do not provide tax, legal or investment advice and should not be represented to customers or the public as financial planners or financial advisors or similar designations.

Introduction

I wrote this book after realizing that my success, and the success of nearly all of my former team members who became Agents, had become a benchmark among all new insurance agents, where seven out of ten struggle to survive.

Very few Agents who left my office had comparable struggles in the field.

As I spoke at more and more training seminars and other gatherings of insurance Agents, I began to see that there was a need for this type of book, a book that opened the doors for new Agents to obtain the levels of productivity and satisfaction that their hard work merits.

I felt that if I didn't address new Agents directly, they would be left to learn from their own mistakes, a very expensive and risky lesson. I even gave this group of common mistakes a name, The New Agent Graveyard (NAG).

I felt that with timely advice, new Agents can avoid the debt that comes with these mistakes. Others just believed this debt was part of the business: "paying your dues." I believe you can avoid the NAG and the debt that comes along with it.

I want to emphasize to new Agents that the most important thing they can do to achieve success lies in their treatment of team members.

I think my approach is different from most because it emphasizes that new Agents should regard themselves first as business owners and not as insurance salespersons. To understand their role as business owners, new Agents must appreciate that this expanded role brings new and very important responsibilities.

New Agents must fully acknowledge that their very first customers are actually their team members. How are you going to treat them? Will you make their dreams come true?

For both new Agents and established Agents who want to raise the bar in their offices, this book presents systems that I think will be easy to install, and once in place, these systems will have an immediate impact on an Agency.

The key to all of this is that Agents should allow their team members to read this book so that the team members can implement these simple procedures.

I believe these systems can almost triple an Agency's production and make the lives of Agent-owners a lot easier.

In Part I, I want people to see the great opportunities in this business. Agents are not like doctors or attorneys who must see their clients. Agents remain available, but their team members can assist with services and other duties to their clients.

This business offers such an amazing lifestyle for the Agent and the Agent's team members.

But new Agents must create a system from the beginning that allows them to enjoy all of the things this industry allows, with all of the benefits of residual income.

Each year, real estate agents start over to make next year's sales. As insurance Agents, we start off the New Year where we left off at the old year. We can pile onto it because it's residual income.

The other feature of this business is that an Agent's team members are licensed in the same way as the Agent. The team members, under the law, can perform the same functions as the Agent.

However, some Companies may have other requirements in addition to licensing in order for team members to assist with sales activities, and Agents should be sure to follow all Company guidelines as well as their states' rules and regulations.

In Part II, I have included systems to find, create, motivate and train your team.

In Part III, I describe a couple of difficult situations that successful new Agents may have to deal with.

In Part IV, I've included an array of short stories about successful Agents who came from a variety of backgrounds. I wanted these stories to serve as the counter argument to those who say they couldn't succeed in this business. I hope each reader of this guide will be able to relate to at least one story in this section and see that your dream can come true no matter what obstacle you might face.

Finally, in Part V, I give you Speedy. This is basically my system that is being used by someone in another type of business. It was this encounter that brought it all home to me that my systems can relate to a lot of businesses.

I believe that if you follow this guide, no matter the business you are in, you are going to be successful.

This book represents the accumulated experiences of a lifetime of learning from so many others. I would like to recognize some of those many for whom I am most grateful:

Darnell Hoskins	Buster Nelson
Eschol Curl	Terry Stone
Tyrice Walker	Norman Thomas
Jim Jay	Melvin Johnson
Willie Walker	Thomas Ntuk
Chris Schell	Peggy Abkemeier
Hans Schell	Bill Mathews
Frank Radaszewski	Michelle Williams
Roosevelt Meuks	Dave Sullivan
John Prusakowski	Chris Martin
Don Gardner	Edwin Young
Barion Mills	Brian Young
Eddie Slay	Cal and Lydia Roebuck
Amos Jefferies	Doug and Brenda Bohannon
Todd Smith	Tracy Blair
Terry Jones	Maya and Oprah

—— AL Sicard

Creating the "A" Team

Making the Decision to Become an Agent

I've been an agent—a very successful training agent—for nearly a decade.

It's great. I love it.

It only seems to get better every year. I don't care what the economy is like or who the President is—it's always been good.

Now, you may want to take the same path and to enjoy the same thrills of leadership, travel, fortune and companionship. It sounds like a dream, but I lived it, and you can, too.

There is the freedom of being an entrepreneur. It's not a 9-to-5 job, and that's just the thing you want from this lifestyle. Once you set up your Agency as I did, you will be free to indulge in the perks: exotic travel, a beautiful home, a luxury car, more time with your loved ones and more opportunities to participate in your favorite pastimes or sports.

You may even feel guilty when you see your friends because they seem to be working harder than you and making less money. Your residual income will keep building with far less work effort. After all, doctors and lawyers must continue to see their clients, but you have trained, educated and motivated team members who have the same license as you to handle the customers' concerns.

Why not make hundreds of thousands of dollars while you have team members run your agency? Use my systems and you can continue to grow your business.

But if you're planning to walk in my shoes—my size 15 shoes—I can tell you this:

Find a job you love, where work is play, and where you have an opportunity to grow and learn from great teachers. Then, make sure you take great care of the people you work with and the customers who keep your business.

That's just good advice for anyone going into business. But this is the insurance business, and you've got to do more.

What I'm telling you is this: Business has a lot of pitfalls that can hurt a new Agent, but there are even more pleasant surprises for someone who wants to be a success.

There are a lot of insurance agents out there—more than 17,000 just in the industry's largest company. Half of them aren't selling insurance anymore. They're just holding onto their books of business. They don't get it. That's how crazy it is.

That's why insurance companies, such as the one I work for, are such great companies. And it's the greatest opportunity to be an Agent-Owner.

It's *the* greatest opportunity.

So, if you're already an Agent, and you haven't brought someone in, that's sad.

Let's see if we can make your life a little bit happier and your wallet a lot plumper.

Let me explain in the following pages.

Owning Your Own Business

How many students in colleges want to be an insurance agent?

Not very many.

But how many students in college want to own their own businesses?

All of them.

It's this stark and simple observation that will lead you to the engine that drives your entire office.

There is no ramrod drillmaster sergeant in my office. There are no automatic bonuses that would make Wall Street bankers blush. In fact, there are barely any bonuses at all.

The members' drive and energy comes from within each of the members I hire for my team. Hey, I've done this more than 100 times in less than 10 years. I can list more than 80 successful agents who passed through my office to join your ranks, and each of them made more than $100,000 the first year out.

Am I lucky? Maybe, but no one is that lucky. I've got a system; and I'm passing it on to you.

You will be looking for these qualities in those you place around you. These people will literally take over the business from you. They have the qualities found in workers such as the co-pilots of the planes you will be riding to exotic vacations.

They can step in whenever needed. They are fully prepared.

These are also the qualities you would want in an heir. So, I also get a lot of Corporate's offspring knocking on my door.

And while you may think a lot of this is blasphemy back in the industry's big corporate offices, I can tell you, it's Corporate that is paying for the books and speakers which train my people. They want agencies that can perform at a high level for more than three to five years.

But always remember that any procedure or system described in this book must align with the guidelines and procedures of both your Company and your state's Department of Insurance.

New Agent Graveyard

How to Avoid It and How to Get Out of It

I believe new Agents develop an addictive relationship with their businesses.

Typically, after three years of enjoying the exhilaration of owning their business and probably seeing some relatively big growth, there comes a huge letdown.

- They are tired.
- They are out of money.
- The hours remain terrible.
- Their personal relationships, especially their marriages, are going sour from inattention. The divorce rate among insurance Agents is startling.
- Their dream homes, the castles they bought or built for their families, are straining their personal finances. There's an epidemic of people out there in severe debt – 90 percent who stay on these paths.

And all the way to this early grave, I hear these new Agents chanting the mantras:

> "Lead by example. If I don't work hard, my workers aren't going to work hard."

And:

> "You have to spend a lot of money to make a lot of money."

Here's another example: These new Agents invariably assign the wrong duties to the people they hire and even to themselves.

They look at their office team, and they think, "I only have service people. I need a salesperson."

They start by assigning themselves most of the sales and all of the marketing responsibilities. They end up spending a large share of their pool of borrowed cash on marketing just to fulfill their self-esteem on the sales side.

These new Agents will go out to make door-to-door sales, cold calls and maybe turn to their personal relationships, their family and friends, for new applications.

Meanwhile, the service people in the office, who are never adequately trained, spend their days taking calls, mistakenly offering incorrect information, misdirecting calls and taking messages for the Agent.

Or they may have a senior team member who hasn't sold anything for the last couple of decades and isn't motivated to go back into the field. They are paying for the love relationships these agents have with their current customers, but there will be no growth or production.

As the new Agent quickly sinks into an abyss of debt, there's never any money reserved to train the service people. They never learn how to pivot, so all of the money that was spent on marketing to drive customers to the Agency's phones gets lost. The customers are stymied by service people who don't have the skills to deal with their customers' immediate needs.

Instead of the old ABC's adage: "Always Be Closing," these untrained team members will "Always Be Chatting." They have no reason to sell.

There are other areas where new Agents just get things backwards.

If you look at team meetings in these agencies, you will see an Agent summon team members together to listen to the Agent lecture for 90 percent of the meeting. And then the Agent walks out before anyone else can step up and say something. Where is the development and two-way communication in that?

* * *

Here are four general observations.

Too many new Agents

- spend too much.
- let their obsession with their Agency ownership destroy their personal relationships.
- become an Agent who is selling rather than remain a business owner who is managing.
- spend money that should be set aside for taxes, leading to gambling at the end of the year on debatable tax deductions and risking an ugly tax audit in the near future.

It's a business. We are business owners. You cannot make those types of mistakes.

Spending

Typically new Agents spend money for things that are not going to bring income. It's the idea of investment versus expenses. They spend for things that just make them feel good.

Almost all new Agents believe they must spend everything they have: the loan from the Company (say $100,000 or more) and the cash they personally invested in the business. They expand and remodel their offices (costing maybe $50,000), wrap their vehicles with custom ads (maybe another $5,000), buy some company icons—teddy bears or whatever— and then go out and hire expensive salespeople.

I've seen Agents buy coffee machines that cost $5,000. They put up signs and billboards that cost thousands of dollars. They sponsor every sports team because those kids have the Company's logo on their backs and these Agents think that's going to bring people to their agency. It doesn't.

All that junk— Hey, look at my Agency pens!—doesn't bring you policies. That helps to brand you. <u>It does not bring you policies</u>.

Spending on advertising is great for the Company, as a whole, but it should be purchased in later years once you have earned considerable profits that can then be used to brand the Agency.

In the early years, a new Agent just cannot afford to advertise because it does not bring in the income that will ensure the success of the Agency.

If the Agent has assumed the mantle of the salesperson for the Agency, when the sales numbers are poor, the Agent instinctively believes he or she must pour more money into marketing. To maintain a book of business, the Company expects a certain level of production, and if it's not met, the entire business is at risk of being taken back.

So you can see that *having one person in charge of marketing and sales presents a clear internal conflict*, and no large company would make the head of its marketing division also the head of its sales division.

In a small business, the Agent must rely on the Advisory Board to impose the fiscal discipline on expenses for marketing. The best way is to show the Advisory Board the business plan and insist that the board not let the Agent go over the set limit.

Otherwise, it can result in devastation. At home the spouses of the new Agents say, "Hey. I didn't know this much would be spent. I was told this amount by my (husband or wife)."

The extra money that is being spent does not come out of the Company's loan. It comes out of the Agent-owner's house, the family car, the kids' education fund. That's the nastiness.

As the family's personal savings is drained, the spouse directs his or her anger at the Company. This is why many insurance companies want to have each couple sit at the table and review the business plan before accepting the opportunity to run an Agency.

The natural reaction of the Agent-owner to a disconcerted spouse will be: "You're not supporting me. It's tough times now, but we're going to be rich later."

Across the table, the spouse is replying, "I'm not seeing it."

And the spouse is correct. I don't see it either.

These new Agents believe everyone else new to the industry dips into their personal savings and spends, spends, spends. But they're wrong. They just don't know it. It's a lack of education. They are not reading the books or speaking to the successful Agents in the country before they enter into the business as an Agent-owner.

Then there is the "competitive syndrome." These competitive types start out doing so well. They love to have their name at the top of the achievement lists. They have to be Number One, and their spending is out of control.

But these people have their credit cards maxed out. They can't enjoy the Company's reward trips because they can't afford to go on the trips at all. They're broke!

These competitive types should not be in charge of the money either. For them, it's an adrenaline rush. Can you imagine a college student or one just out of college with a $100,000 credit line? In their heads, they're thinking, "I've never had money before so I'm going to spend it. BUT, I'll get it back."

It's like gambling. It just feels so good! They impulsively want this, and this and this! They go crazy.

What's to stop them? The Advisory Board can serve that purpose. The Board has the business plan, and spending must be approved by the Board which should include an attorney and a Certified Public Accountant.

You've got to have that "money guy" who steps up and shouts, "You don't have it. Don't spend it."

Your spouse needs to have a relationship with the accountant, too. If additional spending is to happen, it's got to go through the Advisory Board and the spouse has to be informed. That way, there is an agreement about just how far the additional spending will go.

Relationships at Home

The embarrassing aspect of this business is that after you work so hard for two to three years just to get to a point where you don't have to work, you are confronted by the growing stress in your domestic relationship. And it comes in different ways.

The partner who is the Agent is working long hours and focused totally on the business all the time – 24/7 it's all about Agency. There is the stress of leading the team members at work. At times, team members can seem just like having more kids to shepherd through life.

It can be overwhelming to the Agent.

For the Agent's spouse, it is overwhelming, too. The spouse feels as if the relationship has been devalued, lost or shoved aside because the Agency has taken over their lives.

It's similar to what happens to professional sports coaches. The coaches have to spend so many hours on the job, overseeing so many people. It's a good comparison.

There is also the issue of being a celebrity in your community. A spouse must cope with the identity issues that come with that.

It makes me uncomfortable to say this and it should make you uncomfortable to hear about it, but sometimes the old sexual stereotypes can suddenly surface in what started out as a relationship of mutual respect. I wish it were not so, but I have seen this and heard from agents about these extremely difficult circumstances developing among some very modern-thinking individuals.

For some Agents, spouses sometimes become envious of the amount of money the Agents are making at their jobs, but resentful about how much time is being taken away from maintaining the household. These spouses may have had a notion about how their marital relationship would ripen sweetly, and instead, it is souring. They begin to consider themselves as being second to the Agency in the eyes of their loved one.

Interestingly, some spouses who work in the home tend to be more flexible than those who work outside the home. The stay-at-home workers have already accepted the new dynamics of the Agent's relationship, realizing that the relationship must try to accommodate the varied needs of their Agent-owner spouse.

However, for the majority of spouses who are working at their own careers outside the home, having a spouse in Agency often becomes an overwhelming burden.

For example, think about the lifestyle of an Agent-owner. They send you on probably 10 trips a year as rewards, conventions or assignments. And on those trips, spouses typically are introduced at small gatherings in a obligatory manner while the focus of every conversation is about how well their Agent-spouses are performing in the business.

For these couples, I don't really have any answers. It's similar to being married to a professional athlete or a police officer. It's a lifestyle you just have to choose to accept. You have to understand that you are buying into the lifestyle. If you don't enjoy it, you need to talk about that before entering this career. There's no way around it, Agency will take over your lives.

For Agents who are traveling all the time while support is flagging at home, there is always temptation at conventions or on other trips. They meet someone else who is going through the same types of struggles and who may be more empathetic about a fellow agent's travails—at least for that one night.

I wish I could offer a specific system to avoid these devastating consequences for so many Agent-owners and their families.

All I can offer is a very strong recommendation that new Agents make arrangements for marriage counseling at the beginning of their business. Like any prophylactic, I think it could help couples who enter Agency to have a strong relationship with a marriage counselor before any trouble surfaces.

It seems reasonable that there should be a separate "business" plan in place to address problems in the Agent-owner's marriage.

Some Agent-owners use prenuptial agreements because they are making so much money that it becomes a major issue in any relationship.

Later in this book, I recommend mandatory counseling for new hires. Recently, I've expanded my thinking about this, and I believe that counseling should start with the first hire: you and your spouse.

It's no guarantee, but I think it's easy to justify the expense.

As a new Agent, I'm sure you can see it already. Agency is tough and challenging work. It pays to be prepared. You wouldn't go driving across some long, washboard road in Alaska without a spare tire and some tools, would you?

We're in the insurance business. And we should be thinking first about insuring that our families survive what obviously will be an ordeal. The goal here is to make the ordeal worth it at the other end.

Being a Salesperson
When You Must Be a Manager

The people who thought this was sales, sales and more sales, wind up working ridiculous hours and burning themselves out.

It's a far easier path to be a manager who teaches people and works through people to do the job.

If you come into your new Agency as a salesperson, usually your team members are the first to suffer. This configuration destroys Agencies.

Here's what happens: You end up doing the bulk of the work. So you are not really owning an Agency, you've created a job for yourself that really isn't a good job.

This can lead to situations I've seen where an Agency's team members actually earn more than the Agent they work for while they work less than their boss!

As I explained previously, the Agent will spend far too much on marketing while trying to handle all of the sales. The Agent ends up working for the team member.

Take the Tax Breaks
But Don't Take Cash Needed for Taxes

There are two sides to consider when a new Agent addresses taxes.

On one side, there are new Agents who spend so much money that they feel compelled to dip into the money that is supposed to be withheld for taxes.

The most devastating thing that can happen to an Agency is a bad tax audit.

The flip side is that some new Agents spend too much on taxes because they don't want to deal with the record keeping or to take the time to gain an understanding of the tax rules necessary to take the deductions they are entitled to.

An Agent can lose $30,000 a year by not documenting tax deductions permitted by the law. There are Agents who are making $250,000 and other Agents who are making only $180,000 because they don't understand the tax law.

You should understand your taxes as well as your Certified Public Accountant. A C.P.A. is going to give you advice, but they aren't going to tell you how to live your life. Basically, you are doing your taxes.

Both sides of this coin are equally detrimental to a new Agency.

The solution?

I suggest that you find a tax advisor, a C.P.A., who is familiar with your insurance Company. Also, have someone other than yourself do your books. A bookkeeper may be more valuable than a C.P.A.

A bookkeeper will ensure that you have that piece of paper to document what you spent on a trip or a business lunch. If you don't have it, the tax auditor is going to question everything.

Second, pay yourself. You should have a paycheck just like your team members. That way you won't be dipping into the reserves or other accounts where you have no business.

In summary, none of these four heavily trodden paths—spending excessively, ignoring family, selling rather than managing and risking a bad tax audit—will lead to a long-term, thriving Agency, and any of them can lead to your business's early demise. I call these misconceptions the New Agent Graveyard. Don't be a NAG.

Systems to Create an Organization That Works Without You

We sell insurance, right? And what is insurance? It's being financially prepared for the unexpected. I'm sure you've got plenty of insurance to cover you and your loved ones.

But what would happen if you were involved in an accident and could only work an hour a day?

I don't think your parent company puts a replacement agent in there, does it?

So we have to plan for that. What would you do? What would your employees do?

Does that sound like I'm selling insurance? It sure does. I'm selling insurance to you, but it doesn't come from a big insurance company like ours, and you're not going to get any cash out of it—not from your parent company, anyway.

But you will profit from it whether or not something happens to you. It comes from the way you set up your organization and from the people who are sitting right in front of you.

No matter how big or small your Agency is today, it's got to be able to fully function without you.

In a way, as the owner and the top gun in the Agency, you've got to step back.

You've actually got to take a mental leap and believe that for you, **being busy is a form of laziness.**

Let's just think about that.

A lot of people are going to say, "Well, AL's saying, we don't need to be doing all the work."

No! What I'm saying is create the Agency that works totally without you. Have many work for thelf

Once you do that, you're going to stretch what your team members can do and what they're capable of doing. They're going to enjoy it more, too.

So, to have that thing run without you, how many applications can they do without you?

I'm not saying you're not going to work. I'm just saying, what can they do totally without you having any specific, routine jobs to do?

Without you checking email.

Without you setting up an appointment.

How can they totally run the office?

Once you have the office running without you, then you can add yourself to the mix and assign yourself the duties that you are really passionate about.

Don't assign yourself the duties you dislike. Don't take on responsibilities that could lead to stress or burnout. Don't get on the road to NAG.

For All Systems:
I Don't Care What Way We Do It, But That We Do It the Same Way

I love systems. My Agency is nothing but an amalgamation of systems that interlock to make a smooth, money-making machine.

I have systems for

- Training
- Phone quotes
- Home closings
- Setting appointments
- Client retention
- Accountability

Here's an example of what I mean:

Most Agents hate those "conversations" where they have to tell one of their team members that he or she is falling behind or failing to produce. Let's face it, it always becomes a confrontation.

- You are on the offense trying to make your points by fixing responsibility and offering constructive suggestions and criticisms;

- Your team member is on defense, shifting responsibility, rejecting your criticisms and deflecting your suggestions. Even worse, the team member is saying nothing at all, a sign of indifference or bewilderment.

I chose a different path for my Agency to achieve the same goal.

I have a big board in the office. It's called a Scoreboard, and each team member is assigned a different color. To determine who is outperforming and who is falling behind, all I have to do is look at the board when I walk in. If someone's color isn't up there, I know, and he or she knows, the whole office knows—the score.

[margin note: who put the colors up there?]

But I leave it up to the lagging team member to bring it to my attention. It brings a whole new dynamic to the conversation. The stress is transferred from me to the non-performer. From there, we can work together.

[margin note: if they want to do better]

What's incredible about this type of situation is that if those same non-performing team members do not get reviews and are not coached or held accountable, they will come to you for a raise when you feel the need to fire them. And that's just a result of a lack of management on your part.

It's not their fault; it's your fault.

[margin note: to make them want to do better]

AL Sicard's System

**"If you can't market, nothing else matters.
If you *can* market, nothing else matters."**

A top Agent once told me he could sell to 9 out of 10 people who walk into his Agency; the worst agent can sell to 8 out of 10 of those same people.

So this business has nothing to do with sales and everything to do with marketing.

I don't believe in placing a heavy emphasis on advertising.

It's all management.

My system focuses on

- Lead generation
- Lead conversion
- Retention rate

My system uses low-cost, recent college graduates, college interns and high school students. I offer them the opportunity to have the

"Entourage" lifestyle portrayed in the HBO hit about Hollywood stardom entrancing the young newbies:

- a clear, quick path to business ownership
- clear, quick training
- challenging workloads with clear goals
- independence, personal responsibility and personal growth
- a step-by-step approach to achieving their goals
- fair competition and immediate recognition

My system delivers

- a focused, highly motivated, cohesive work force
- high turnover that generates a "positive" atmosphere
- huge numbers of applications for insurance
- loyal customers who grow into friends
- miniscule overhead
- fewer headaches for everyone
- a path to becoming a community leader

I hire team members with the goal of making them the owner of a highly profitable business in just a couple years. I recruit motivated youths directly out of college and even from the ranks of high school teens.

but how does he make money?

I train each of them in three days to work in a well-defined job with clear assignments of responsibilities that do not require my intervention. Everyone gets the same training before I assign them specific tasks.

I use high school teens and college interns as Agent Contact Representatives (ACRs) to generate leads for my Agency's system. Each employee receives the same training, but the arrangement allows each level of the system— "agents," student interns and part-time, high school workers—to develop expertise for specific tasks.

After two years of work and hired at staggered intervals, these "agents-in-training" are departing every six months to a year to become insurance Agents, licensed and fully capable of striking out on their own. Meanwhile, I am bringing in fresh, young recruits eager to move up the training agency's ladder.

In addition, some persons come for a three-month stint to train and observe. But either way, my most senior team members mentor the new team members.

I played a lot of basketball in school, and my Agency feels more like a college basketball team than an insurance agency. New hires straight out of training jump at the opportunity to write 100 or more applications each month, all in the pursuit of their dreams to become business owners.

How Most Insurance Agencies Are Organized

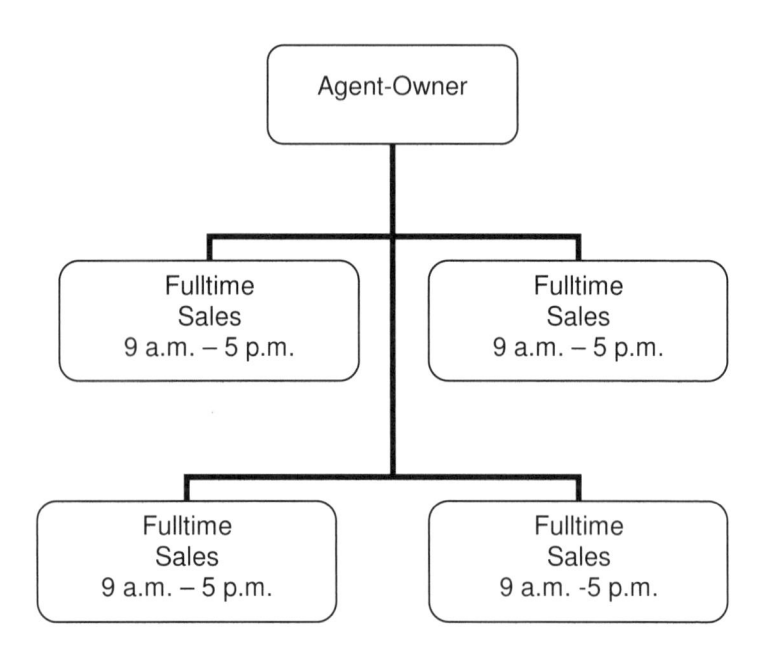

```
                    ┌─────────────┐
                    │ Agent-Owner │
                    └─────────────┘
                           │
         ┌─────────────────┼─────────────────┐
         │                 │                 │
┌─────────────────┐        │        ┌─────────────────┐
│    Fulltime     │        │        │    Fulltime     │
│     Sales       │        │        │     Sales       │
│ 9 a.m. – 5 p.m. │        │        │ 9 a.m. – 5 p.m. │
└─────────────────┘        │        └─────────────────┘
                           │
         ┌─────────────────┴─────────────────┐
┌─────────────────┐                 ┌─────────────────┐
│    Fulltime     │                 │    Fulltime     │
│     Sales       │                 │     Sales       │
│ 9 a.m. – 5 p.m. │                 │ 9 a.m. -5 p.m.  │
└─────────────────┘                 └─────────────────┘
```

How AL's System Is Organized

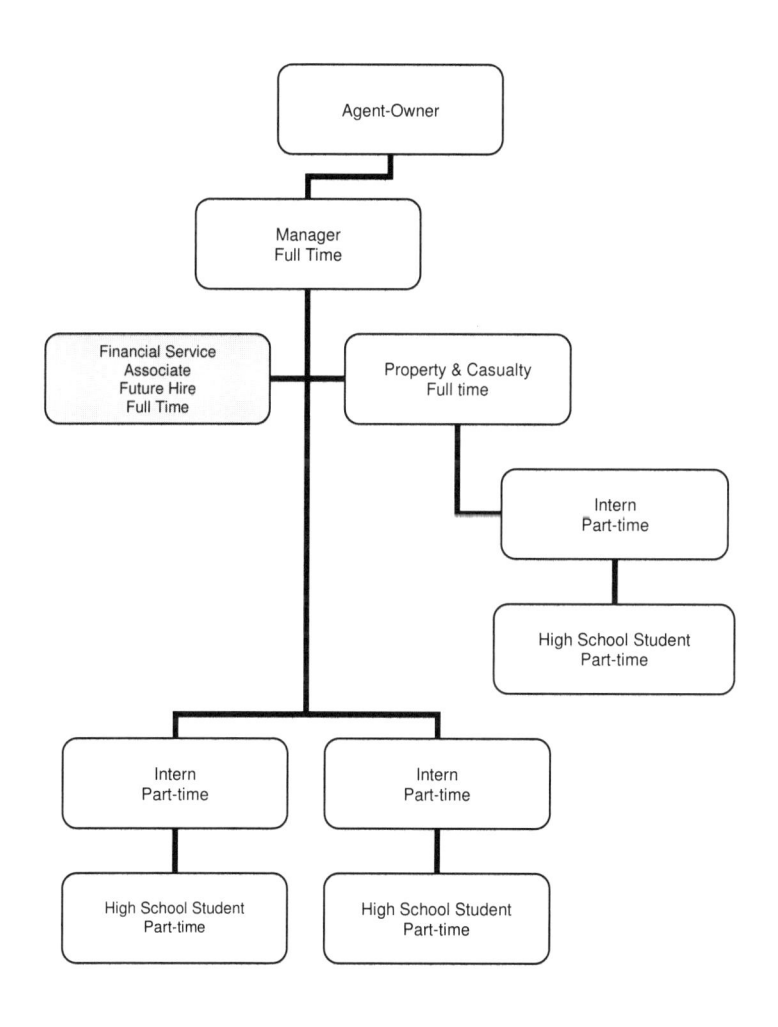

- Agent-Owner
  - Manager Full Time
    - Financial Service Associate Future Hire Full Time
    - Property & Casualty Full time
      - Intern Part-time
        - High School Student Part-time
    - Intern Part-time
      - High School Student Part-time
    - Intern Part-time
      - High School Student Part-time

Leads

In my system, there are only three ways I pay to generate leads:

- Internet leads
- Postcards
- Telemarketing

Referrals don't cost me anything. To generate leads, my team members run their own telemarketing.

Every night, after the Agency closes at 5:00 o'clock, each "agent's" team of ACRs gets a list of phone numbers to call for about an hour. At each contact by phone, an ACR reads from a tested script with the goal of getting 2-4 quotes each night. Once the ACR obtains basic information for a quote, the phone call ends. The ACR is trained to use the computer to prepare the quotes and to present the quotes to the licensed team member.

If you just get the vehicle information, you can send the quote. And what type of quote would you send? The best quote.

Now some of these customers will call back as soon as they get their quote. Some will think it's a mistake. But don't be concerned that they will be mad if the final price you give them is higher than the initial quote. They've seen commercials that claim to save $400. I've never saved $400; they haven't either. They understand marketing, and they're smarter about saving than any Agent I know. Even if they save a smaller amount, they will still view it as helpful.

AL's Marketing Funnel

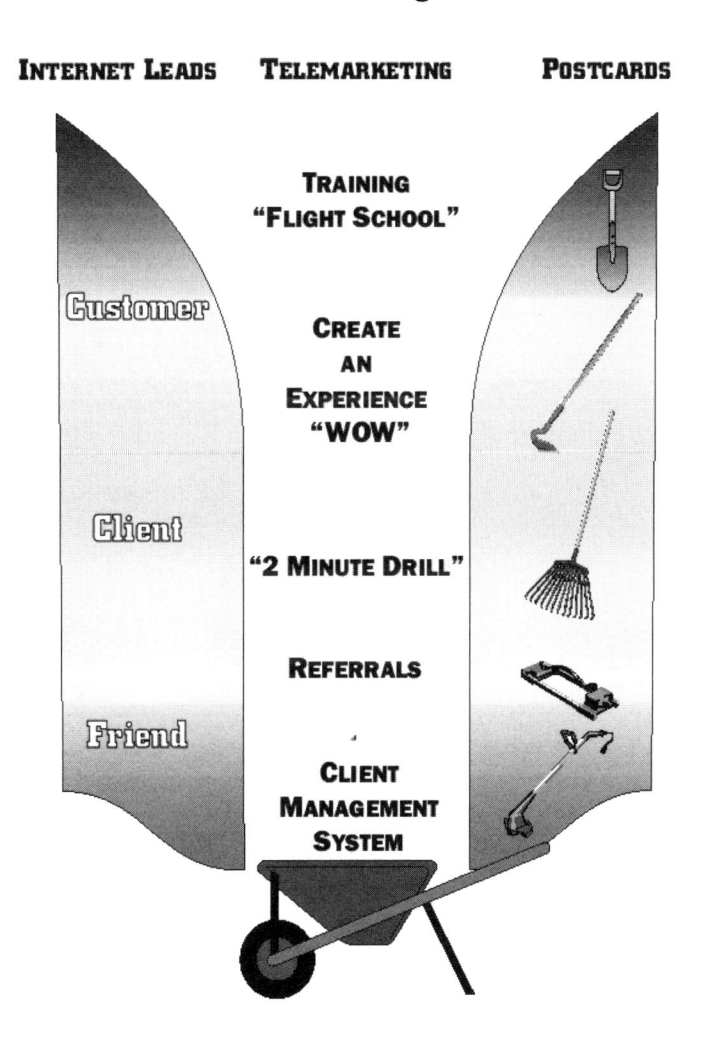

INTERNET LEADS   **TELEMARKETING**   **POSTCARDS**

Customer

TRAINING
"FLIGHT SCHOOL"

CREATE
AN
EXPERIENCE
"WOW"

Client

"2 MINUTE DRILL"

REFERRALS

Friend

CLIENT
MANAGEMENT
SYSTEM

A Note About Compliance:
"Don't let what you can't do interfere with what you can do"

Non-licensed team members are the most cost-effective people in your office. Each team member has an assistant. Those assistants are the callers.

When I first started, I had one team member, and three telemarketers (part-time college freshmen and sophomores) who made the calls. The part-time team members received the same training as the full-time team members, but the part-timers understood that while they made calls, they could not present coverages or sign applications. We had 364 applications within three months. In more recent years, I have had three college interns and three part-time high school students who call from 5 to 8 p.m.

How can one salesperson who works 9-5 compete with three telemarketers who work part-time after 5 o'clock? After 5 p.m., people are home. Instead of answering machines, there are live people to talk to.

Any duties of the unauthorized team member must align with the guidelines and limitations that both your Company and your state's Department of Insurance have regarding unlicensed team members.

Retention and Referrals

You might think that lead conversion comes next in this process—the customer is walking in and your team member is selling—but I'm already a step ahead of you.

By the time a customer arrives at my door, my team members are focusing on retention because we're nearly certain that we'll make a conversion. We've done the work ahead of time. Even if we don't convert, we want each person who walks in to come back, bring a friend or send a friend. I want all of my customers to be impressed from the moment they step out of their cars into the Agency's parking lot.

I emphasize ten points my team members must perform, such as greeting our customers with free valet car washes as they arrive at the office and having all documents fully prepared and ready for signatures. This brings a "Wow" factor to each customer's perspective. Such an initial impression is hard to forget, and it plays a pivotal role in customer retention.

In tracking performance, I also consider multi-lining a customer as retention. In my office, "Agents," not the ACRs or clerical team members, answer the phones during the business hours. From that vantage point, they can pivot to add or bundle more policies for the customer.

Lead Conversion

Here's where lead conversion comes into play. Most Agents miss this opportunity.

Once the lead is recorded, my team members run the same play:
- The customer is scheduled for an appointment.
- Call backs from my team members gather every essential detail before the appointment day.
- A suggestion is made to the customers to bring in all of their policies and financial information.
- All documents are prepared and arranged on the desk when the customer walks in the door so my team member can focus on the customer's financial picture, appropriate needs, questions and reservations. Policies are explained in "Baby Terms," which I will address in a later chapter. When customers understand something as complex as insurance or finance, they talk about it, not just with you, but with their friends and relatives. And that leads to referrals.

It runs like a football drill. In fact, it is a drill, and I call it "The 2-Minute Drill." It has 10 points. It never varies. And it works.

The 2-Minute Drill

In football, 75 percent of the points are scored in four key minutes of the game—the last two minutes of the second and fourth quarters. The reason scoring is clustered is that football teams always practice the 2-Minute Drill, over and over again.

The 2-Minute Drill in my Agency is focused on creating "The Experience" for the customer. I'm going for that moment that will stick with them weeks, months and even years after their first visit to my office. It's like "first impression" on steroids.

This drill has ten parts. It never varies, and everyone in the Agency knows it by heart:

1. Order leads. We get these lists from vendors, and they are targeted at specific groups: persons celebrating their 50th birthdays, seniors graduating from high school or single mothers who are younger than 25 years old. We target these groups and others because our Company offers substantial discounts to members of these groups.

2. Telemarketing. Using part-time high school students and college interns, we try to generate two to six leads each hour.

3. From the leads we receive, our goal is to make 15 quotes over the phone or to schedule seven appointments each day. In either case, we prepare a packet for each customer and place an Agency business card with our 800-number on top.

4. For customers who received quotes, we follow up with calls and offer to schedule appointments. For customers with scheduled appointments, we send out postcards that confirm their appointments.

5. The night before every scheduled appointment, we call the customers again. We ask for any missing information needed to fill out the applications in advance of their arrival. And we make sure that our team member confirms that each customer received the quote. Our team member also must reassure the customer with a remark such as "The quote looks great!" The next question is actually more of a directive to each customer. We suggest that they "dust off your other insurance policies and bring them in for a free review." Finally, our team member asks the customer or couple about their preferred beverages so that these will be on the desk at the time we meet.

6. For customers who have a current policy with our Company, at the appointed time, we have a uniformed, car-

wash attendant waiting to greet them when they pull into the office parking lot. Customers receive a free, full-service car wash while they are meeting with our team member. The team member reviews the policies using "Baby Terms" that I'll describe later. The procedure for filing a claim is reviewed. To avoid any confusion that my team would be directly involved in a claim, each customer receives a photograph of the claims team. Customers also receive a quality commitment sheet that basically states: "If we don't have it, you don't need it."

7. After customers leave our Agency, we send them questionnaires. These ask about their level of satisfaction with our services and inquire about the type of gift they would prefer in exchange for any referrals to our Agency.

8. A few days later, we follow up with another call to the customers to encourage completion of the questionnaires. We compile the responses to these questionnaires and post the results in the Agency office.

9. Next, we send a request to customers seeking referral letters from them.

10. Finally, as a thank you for their referrals, whether we received a referral or not, we send them a movie-rental gift certificate or another type of gift.

If You See It or Hear It, Record It

In my office, everything is automatically recorded.* Digital video cameras record everything in the main office and digital audio recorders memorialize every word from every phone call made into my office or made from my office.

I never use these recordings for discipline. I use them to train and recognize my team members.

To prepare my new hires, we record simulated interviews with customers both in person and over the phone. We also record presentations of business plans.

When my team members leave to become Agents elsewhere, they take a copy of their collected recordings with them. I call it their Flight Book, but it's actually a DVD containing their best work. I keep the original in my office. I have a library of them—56 at last count—to use to train my new interns.

* *If you are considering the use of similar recording devices in your office, first check your state laws regarding the use of these devices. Some states have more restrictions than others.*

Everything is in the Flight Book: practice interviews, a recitation of a life plan and best interactions with customers.

I learned this from observing and participating in competitive sports. I played varsity basketball at an NCAA Division I school, the University of Dayton. Whether you are playing at the high school, college or professional level, you will be watching video recordings of your performance. I brought this excellent training method into an insurance office.

All of my phones are recorded. I also have the ability to listen in on phone calls between my team members and customers. This setup allows me to whisper over the phone to my team member without the customer overhearing me.

For example, during a phone conversation, I may listen in and whisper, "This is a great time to introduce such-and-such product."

When team members in my office believe they have achieved a break-through interview, they note the time of the day and pass it to a part-time high school student. These assistants then fetch the recorded conversation from our computerized files and include it in a "Top Ten Plays" collection that we review each week in our meetings. The recording can also be added to the team member's personal Flight Book.

Impressions

In whatever you do, whether it's the service you provide or the way you set up your office, make sure there is a "Wow" factor—something that will grab people's attention and make them notice that you've sweated the details.

The one thing Oprah taught me more than anything else is that it is all about your team.

"Take down all that (company product logo) junk in your office and put up success. People are attracted to success," she said. "Create a vision board of success."

You can get success-type products from your Company.

I took down all of my product posters. I wanted to see my team members' achievements on my wall. I'm not talking about bowling trophies. I wanted to see depictions of their achievements of the goals that were first laid out in their vision boards.

Scoreboard

Each team member has a color. We keep score.

When I go to the scheduling board, I look at colors. If I don't see someone's color up there, to me, that means you don't want to work in my office. I use colors on appointment schedules and application reports. It's embarrassing for a team member to not have his or her color prominently displayed on those public boards. It's like keeping score in front of everyone.

I view basketball, and most sports, as the greatest business training in the world. On a basketball team, your mistakes are published in the local newspaper. If that isn't accountability, what is?

On every basketball team I played on, we kept score. But we scored more than just the point totals. We scored block outs and rebounds. If I wasn't getting my numbers for rebounds, then we worked on rebounds all week.

Numbers don't lie. They don't play favorites.

But I don't use them for discipline.

If someone in my office is taking 60 calls and pivoting on just a third of them while everyone else is pivoting on 84 percent, the team member must bring that to my attention so that we can do some individual training in that area.

Let me just take a moment to explain what I consider to be a successful "pivot."

A successful pivot is not how many policies were written. It is about how the team member tried to engage the customer.

When a policy holder calls my Agency to report the purchase of a new car, I expect my team member to ask that caller if they have life insurance and whether they would like an additional quote in consideration of a multi-line discount. Most customers will appreciate the additional quote.

The idea is to get a receptive customer to look at a quote in a different line. It does not matter if a customer declines. I just want the offer in front of each of them. If nothing else, it makes our customers aware that we offer the product, and they will keep us in mind in the future.

If I have a team member taking 60 calls in the office each week, I can sell far more applications for policies than if that same person is going door-to-door selling policies or making cold calls.

Every time my team members take a service call, I expect them to pivot. All Agent-owners say they do this, but no one monitors it as I do in my Agency. Every day, we monitor the number of calls taken and the number of pivots performed. We always try to reach a pivot rate of 80 percent.

My scoring system removes the onus of bringing up corrective actions from Agent-owners. I require my team members to bring their shortcomings to me. This addresses accountability, an issue that new Agents often choose to ignore or set aside until they are dealing with a situation that is threatening the entire business.

If a team member isn't meeting a number that I've set for performance standards, I want that person to take the initiative and write me a memorandum that identifies the shortcoming and explains why it is happening.

For example, the note might say: "AL, for the last week, I haven't made pivots on 80 percent of my calls. Here's why it happened. In conclusion, they spell out a plan to change it."

This makes my team members come to me about problems they are having. Without this system, these conversations never take place because Agents just hate to bring up these issues until it's too late.

Remember, all of this is running without me. I don't have to be there.

And it runs that way because when I built my systems, I tried to think of each thing that could go wrong. Then I created a system to prevent it or to deal with it.

It took me three months of research and plenty of thought to develop a handbook and a procedures DVD, we call it "The Play Book," that I could hand to my first hire.

When you have that, your new team members start work with very favorable impressions of you.

The Quote

How much time should you spend teaching your team members how to quote? How to quote over the phone?

I dedicate at least 10 hours of video recording to this skill.

For a customer coming in for a specific policy, we may schedule the appointment a week in advance.

Under my system, everything flows from the team member who closed that customer to his or her assistant.

The assistant

- fills out the applications
- sends out a postcard confirming the appointment
- schedules the appointment on the board
- credits the person who took the call by placing that person's **color** on the scoreboard

On the evening before the scheduled meeting, a non-licensed person from my office calls that customer.

The conversation might go like this:

> "Just calling to confirm your appointment. We need a couple pieces of information. The names of the beneficiaries.
>
> "And could you please bring all of your policies in? Just dust everything off—Everything you have. It's just for a review.
>
> "Is there anything you'd like to drink for the appointment? Any questions you have?"

When our customers arrive in our parking lot, they're always met by a car wash attendant. He wears a special shirt and has been paid in advance to give their vehicle a first-class cleaning, inside and out. The car wash is located next to my Agency building. We don't tell our customers about it until they arrive.

A lot of customers will come in, literally sticking just their heads through the door, asking:

"Uh, this guy out there says—is he with you? He wanted to take my car for a car wash. Is that true?"

"Yeah," my team member will say nonchalantly.

"I'll be right back." And we get smiles from our customers before they've even stepped inside the office.

So, the scene is set and our customer returns as a client, which is better than a customer, or it may be even better, because they become a friend by the end of the process.

Once inside our office, the first thing our customers see is their names on our board. It's an electronic board.

"Welcome to the Agency," it says.

On the licensed Agent's desk, all policies are filled out and sitting in front of the customer.

Invariably, my training agents object to this level of preparation. They insist the customer will still buy the policy even if it takes a little extra time filling in the forms while the customer waits.

It's true that the customer usually is there to do business. But my goal is not getting that one application filled out; and it is not getting five to six applications signed at one time.

The goal, at this point, is to get the referral.

Any customer who is forced to sit down and watch you turn your back on them, after giving you all of that information in advance, will not be happy. They will be looking at their watches. And maybe, probably, they're going to buy the policy, but only because they hate shopping for insurance. But they will not be happy if they have to go through that, too. Not only will they be unhappy, but they won't be referring anyone either.

The goal is the referral.

So everything is sitting there and waiting on the desk.

Selling

When I'm interviewing someone for a position on my team, I'll ask them: "Sell me that pen," pointing to one lying on my desk.

That person will always begin by describing the pen in hand: "It's a retractable ballpoint, enclosed in an attractive, marbled barrel with black ink that dries fast."

But I don't sell. In this business, we don't sell.

People buy.

People don't like to be sold; but **people love to buy**.

So all anyone in this business has to do is ask the customer, "What would you like to have in a pen? What else do you like in a pen? Tell me more. Here's this pen, and here are some of the things in the pen that you were looking for."

Baby Terms

For each customer, our licensed Agent reviews each policy using what I call "Baby Terms:"

- Liability is lawsuit protection.
- Medical payments: Friends suing Friends. You don't want your friends suing you. You don't want to be the soccer Mom and no kids are allowed in your car.
- Collision. We just pay the amount above the deductible. If there is $2,000 in damages, and the deductible is $500, we pay $1,500. If you can find a place that negotiates a cheaper repair, you may save yourself some money.

We approach the conversation with confidence, assuming that we will sell the fire insurance policy that the customer asked for when the first contact was made.

Then, we begin probing for additional customer needs. We ask: "Is there anything in your household worth $1000 or more that you're concerned about—such as a computer?"

"Yeah, I got a Dell," your customer will probably say. And that leads us to this little dance:

"Great, we'll put it on a separate policy with no deductible. Is there anything else you want on that policy? Jewelry? Furs? Anything."

And there's your extra application.

Next we ask, "Do you want $1 million or $2 million on the umbrella?"

Most of our customers visiting us for the first time don't know what an umbrella policy is. As the professional, the licensed team member painstakingly explains every detail and all of its ramifications as well as the security it brings.

After the customer leaves the office, we send out a survey to the customer's home. Finally, on the day after the meeting, a non-licensed team member calls to inquire: "How did you enjoy your experience?"

With this system, my Agency averages 2.2 referrals for every customer. About 16 new customers sit down with us each month while their vehicles are being washed.

We try so hard because we know, if we get them, we're getting our referrals. Which means we don't have to spend as much on what?

Marketing.

Complaints:
Focus On the Important Few

If there is a complaint while I am away, it goes on a red sheet.

On that red sheet of paper is

- a description of the complaint
- an account of the team member's efforts to resolve it
- an indication of the result of the team member's efforts
- a recommendation about how we can prevent more complaints of the same type

This is for any complaint, big or small, long-winded or a quip.

For example, here is a dialogue that probably happens all the time in Agents' offices:

Caller: "Is AL there?"

Team Member: "Ah, no. AL's out of town right now. Is there something we can help you with?"

Customer: "Oh God. He's always gone."

There! Did you catch it? That's a complaint.

I need it on a red sheet, and I've got to call that person.

Any little complaint is on that red sheet.

I want it.

They are all a priority. And, of course, big-time clients always have big-time complaints.

Don't Take Complaints

When I'm in the office and a customer calls asking for me, my team members know what to do before I even hear about it.

If it is a question or a complaint, I want my team member to

- Investigate—What does the caller really want?
- Decide if the caller actually wants me on the phone.
- Give me a recommendation before you hand me the phone.

Another way to present this to your team is by using the technique Feel-Felt-Found: I understand how you **feel**; I've **felt** that way before; Here's what I've **found**.

If your team members are trained to follow this procedure, soon you will stop getting most of those calls. They will handle it without you.

Also, non-licensed team members who are part-time should attend a class that explains how to handle customers who make monthly payments. They should be instructed to be patient with these people and skilled in answering all of their questions. The part-time team members are able to spend more time with these customers, to retrieve payment histories, in interpret changes in bills and to explain how the system works. This extra time and effort prevents future complaints and it reassures customers that they are receiving fair treatment.

This is important because you don't want your full-time people stressed out over service issues, each of which can take an hour or longer to resolve.

McDonald's
Consistency and Routines

To build your Agency, it may help to imagine what it would be like to build a McDonald's.

McDonald's is "push button." It's simple and nearly paperless. Everyone does it the same way.

Another thing about McDonald's restaurants: I've never met an owner there, have you?

When it comes to establishing procedures for the Agency, I have one important rule that I mentioned previously, but let me remind you again:

I don't care what way we do it, but that we do it the same way.

Office Decorum

When an Agent is out of the office, it's important that the office maintain its regimen. **Every desk in my office is organized the same way.**

My team members do not keep anything on top of their desks.

They work on one thing at a time.

If I see a pile on the desk, I will burn it.

A pile means stress. I call a pile "a Weed." A pile is like a weed because it will grow. And that causes stress. Just like pulling weeds, we have to get rid of piles on desks. I have no idea what's in any pile and neither does that team member.

There are four folders on each desk:
- Incoming
- Outgoing
- Route and file
- Priority

I will fire anyone who drops some work on someone else's desk. Work always goes in the desk's Incoming Folder.

I was in the The President's Class at Aileron, a local, non-profit, business management school, when Dave Sullivan, president and managing partner of a Denver management consulting firm, recalled this instructional story:

> A well-known CEO once spotted a pile on the desk of one of his vice presidents. So, he quietly took out a blank piece of paper, and on it, he wrote: "Come see me when you get this." And he put it in the middle of the pile.

I would not want to be going to that meeting.

No piles on the desk.

Team Meetings

I have two meetings a week: one for sales and a shorter meeting for service issues where we discuss only the "Red Sheets," the papers where team members record customer complaints and concerns.

There is always an agenda. Everyone is always involved in the presentations and discussions. It's fast-paced. And it's always video-recorded. In case I can't be there, I can review the recording as soon as I return.

At each meeting, one of the team members takes the official notes of the meeting. More recently, I installed voice-recognition software that can automatically transcribe what team members said at the meetings. It transcribes with about 85 percent accuracy—enough for me to get the gist of everything that was discussed.

Team meetings are for the Team. As an owner, be quiet and listen.

These team meetings are about discovering what your team has learned and how they are thinking in your office.

Let your team members talk about the lines of business and what needs to happen next. Have them act like Agents. They should be running the meetings.

Each team member is a generalist with a specialization, such as homeowners insurance. If I or another team member need some additional advice or insight into homeowners insurance, there is a go-to team member who can help.

And at every team meeting, all team members should have something to say about their areas of specialization and how their remarks relate to maxing out the Company's programs and bonuses. They put on the show while I listen and gauge how well they are developing into Agents.

I encourage team members to take the initiative so they will usually assign one of themselves to make the extra effort to find a "guest speaker" for the meeting. This involves contacting someone in another Agency who has expertise in an area of interest to the team. Arrangements are made for a 10-15 minute exchange over a speaker phone. Perhaps someone offers pointers about sales techniques.

Each of my team members has a responsibility to coordinate a team meeting. The recorded meeting is included in the team member's Flight Book as evidence of their leadership skills. It may also produce a highlight for the "Top Ten Plays" DVD.

Perfect Day

I arrange to have Agent visitors come to my office on a "Perfect Day," when we try to generate as many applications as we possibly can. We pull out all the leads that we didn't get to during the week, and we try to get through as many as possible in one day.

The concept of "Perfect Day" first dawned on me long before I knew I wanted to be an Agent. I was in high school, playing basketball in 1989, when I was invited to play in the McDonald's All-American game in New York City.

There were a couple days of practices and scrimmages before the game. We had not yet met coach Bob Knight, and we were just running suicides during one of the early practices.

Suicides are exhausting drills that require each player to run back and forth across the basketball court, touching boundary lines that are progressively farther apart each time. We start at one end of the court and run to the foul line, then back to the end of the court. Then we spin around and run to the half-court line, and back again. Then we run to the farthest foul line and return. Finally we run to the other end of the court and race back.

On that day, we were running at about 80 percent of our capabilities. Finally Bob Knight came in, and he basically asked us to run one suicide as hard as we could—100 percent.

Each of us was trying to impress him, so we ran as hard as we could. When we finished, Knight, obviously not too impressed, yelled: "Now run the rest that way." And he walked out.

With that simple gesture, each of us immediately understood that Bob Knight was only going to accept 100 percent. If you didn't give him 100 percent all the time, you weren't going to play.

That experience made a huge impression on me. When I was developing motivational systems for the team members in my Agency, I wanted them to have that same level of enthusiasm.

I believed we could achieve that level of enthusiasm if we could schedule one day when we just focused on all the things that we try to do well. In other words,

- Pivot on every client and ask about other areas of insurance.
- Run all of the systems that we have when we're quoting over the phone or when a customer enters our office.
- Explain each policy's coverage in the simplest "Baby Terms," to ensure the customers understand what they are getting for their money.

I wanted my team members to attempt just to do it the right way every time for an entire day. I believe this can work for any business that you manage.

In sports: basketball, football, tennis, gymnastics. In performances on the stage or in concert with a piano or guitar, or just giving a speech—in almost any endeavor—there is always that special time where you are "In the Zone." That's what we're trying to elevate our team members to on a "Perfect Day."

Watch the last minutes of any sporting event and the players are playing at their maximum best. The Perfect Day gives you the same pressure situation as that last-minute situation in a game. It gives your team members the confidence and knowledge that they have pushed themselves beyond their limits, and they know what it will take the next time. That's why Perfect Day creates a winning culture. I believe you create a winning culture so that in the last minutes they can push themselves to their best.

On the appointed day, I bring a large time clock to the office—kind of like a game clock—and we set it up to countdown those eight hours while we really put into action perfect execution of what I'd been teaching the whole year. Once you've stretched yourself, and done it that way, it's hard to go back.

If a team member has made 60 contacts and pivoted 60 times, that's a perfect day whether or not additional applications were taken. And it's really fun. It puts some pressure on the team, and it creates some peer pressure in the office because everyone wants to perform well in front of their co-workers.

And then there are the records that team members set. We achieved 102 applications one day not too long ago.

Several other Agencies have attempted to beat that record and that has produced several Perfect Days for them.

When the day is done, and the records are announced, we take a breather and reconsider what Bob Knight was trying to tell me and my fellow basketball players two decades ago: Don't restrict yourself to one day or one practice or one drill that is perfect and takes 100 percent effort. By achieving perfection on this one day, it shows everyone that we can continue to have those "Perfect" days throughout the year.

Hey! Be at your best! Push yourself to the edge, and I think once you do that, you never really go all the way back.

I can't overestimate the level of excitement these Perfect Days create. And this really makes it fun because for one day, we focus on all the little things we need to do. And it brings about a culture in the office that the team members understand: "This is what we are about. This is what we need to do."

And they remember it for the entire year.

Stress Buster

Sometimes a high-maintenance policy holder can drive your whole office crazy.

These incidents can drain your team members before they're finished drinking their morning coffee: trying to explain for the sixth time why a payment was adjusted; making special arrangements for a late payment; dealing with a frequently confused and angry customer.

I have a system for this. The goal is to train my customers about the procedures of the monthly payment plans.

For each of the relatively small number of customers in this special category, we channel them. We herd them. We insist that they not call us until after three o'clock when we will be able to take the time to tell them what happened to their account in the past, the present and the future.

And we caution them that if they call any earlier in the day, we're going to have some issues.

I'm dead serious.

We're doing that customer a favor because he or she wants to pay a different way than everyone else.

And it's worked great. Because my most important person—that young, energetic team member—does not want that monthly payment plan call because it can just ruin the whole day.

Advisory Board
Mentors, Teachers and Coaches

It's expensive to learn from your mistakes. But it costs you nothing to learn from someone else's mistakes.

That's why I always ask new Agents: Who is on your Advisory Board?

Everyone needs to have an Advisory Board because when you go through Agency, you do the stupidest things you can imagine. You must have people who you can call on. They will knock some sense into you.

And for new agents, you should have a Million Dollar Round Table recipient on your Advisory Board. You can make MDRT by luck, or you can have someone that's an MDRT member train you. Those are the only two ways I know you can get there. The opportunities don't just come out of the blue. It's the same people every year. You've got to have them on your Board so you have someone teaching you the easiest way to do things.

If you don't have this Advisory Board, you're spending a lot of money that you didn't have to spend.

When I formed my first Advisory Board, I sought the top Agents in the Company and an array of other professionals. I would ask them about problems I was having, and they would give me better answers than my peers in the business.

My first Advisory Board had

- Frank Radaszewski of Vandalia, Ohio. He's a great Life Agent. At that time, I wanted to know everything about life insurance.

- Barion Mills of Rochester, N.Y., who is a top all-around Agent and a great disciplinarian.

- Clay Mathile, who grew Iams Pet Foods into an international brand. I met Clay through his sons who were in high school with me. After I graduated from the University of Dayton, Clay also accepted me at his state-of-the-art business school, Aileron, based in Tipp City, just north of Dayton, Ohio.

- Richard J. Chernesky, a first-rate corporate attorney at Dinsmore & Shohl, LLP in Dayton. Clay introduced me to Dick, who gave me advice about taxes, human resources and how to handle the money that was coming through my business.

- Greg Truesdell of Middletown, Ohio, a veteran agent. His daughter was in high school when she trained me about how to run systems and how to quote.

- Matt Schomburg of Texas is the best telemarketer. He developed "shot-calling."

- DC Clement of Bowling Green, Ky. He helped me in the capacity of a "success mentor" in dealing with both celebrity status and wealth.

- Melvin Johnson of Memphis, Tenn., and Terry Stone of Nashville, Tenn. They taught me how to max out our Company's scorecard and how to get the most out of the Company's bonus plans.

- "Famous" Amos Jefferies of Dayton. He taught me how to brand myself and the Agency.

- Terry Jones of Nashville, Tenn. He opened the door and explained the Company's culture to me.

- Todd Smith of Dickson, Tenn. He is the most talented Agent I have met.

The most recent additions to my Advisory Board are

Dr. Maya Angelou, an actress, performing dancer, author and civil rights activist. She was the inaugural poet for President Bill Clinton's first term. She is the author of "I Know Why the Caged Bird Sings" (1977), a three-time Grammy winner for the spoken word (1993, 1995, 2002) and recipient of the Presidential Medal of the Arts (2000) and the Lincoln Medal (2008). She was the "Northern Coordinator" for Dr. Martin Luther King Jr.'s Southern Christian Leadership Conference until his assassination.

Raymond J. McGuire, a Wall Street banker and finance expert, born in my hometown of Dayton. In July 2009, he was named sole head of Citigroup's global investment banking. Before joining Citigroup in 2005, he was global co-head of Morgan Stanley's mergers and acquisitions unit. In October 2006, Black Enterprise Magazine featured him as one of the most powerful Blacks on Wall Street.

Award vs. Reward

Most Agents would rather pay bonuses and brag about bonuses than recognize their team members for a job well done.

> But what publication are your team members featured in?
> Team members are salespeople. But what awards do they get?
> What have you done to recognize your team members?
> What career path does your team member have in the organization?

I try to see my business through the eyes of my team members. If they see the Agent as someone who is just running around, plugging holes, trying to do everything and anything, well, they are not seeing a leader, are they?

And if they don't see a leader, that Agent is not going to be able to get the best people as team members.

Good team members become frustrated when the Agency does not have direction, a handbook or a procedures manual.

One consequence is that after team members are hired, it becomes difficult to fire them because they were never trained which is why they aren't performing to expectations.

So where should the new Agent point the new Agency?

Go after the Company's Awards. Have team members create and maintain procedures manuals with the objective of winning a specific Company award.

If you can win the Awards, that will lead to the Reward of more money flowing into your business.

At my Company, there are the industry Awards for such areas as exotic traveling, clubs recognized by the Company's top officers and even the Super Bowl. Chase those with a vengeance. Your team will get caught up in it, too.

Newsletters

We publish a newsletter in my office. It's created on a computer and delivered over the internet.

We send it to our Company's management.

We send it so my team members get recognized. **You want your team members to get recognized**. It's the step after you have introduced them to the Management Office. Later, I'll explain more about new hires.

This also motivates everyone to strive to be Agents.

Team members will take pride in being recognized on the front page of the newsletter. I've found that they make more effort to achieve that recognition than to get more money in their paycheck.

But where does that recognition lead? It better lead them to something better.

So, where's the growth within your Agency?

What if some of your team members are hesitant about trying to become Agents? I know a lot of people are like that, and a lot of

Agents feel their team members aren't aspiring for a top job somewhere.

Let me talk to those reluctant team members for 10 minutes, and I'll bet they will want to be an Agent. Give me 10 minutes. And if you don't want to hire me to come to your office, well, just show them the first few pages of this book!

The publication of the office newsletter has become so ingrained in my team members that the trained Agents who are now working at their own Agencies send me newsletters that they have produced. These publications also motivate my team members.

Branding

Don't use money to brand yourself.

Branding can wait several years until after you've established your business. I brand by having my team members participate in community service.

At the beginning, new Agents want to put their face out there to brand it. I think you need to be good first, and build the brand around that. A brand implies that you are good at something.

So establish yourself first, and then brand yourself.

You can brand with community service, presentations at schools and churches, home seminars and participation in the centers of influence of the community, such as the mayor or leaders of influential and highly visible organizations.

All these paths to branding have one thing in common, you don't pay for them. They are free and helpful to your business.

Fire Someone

"You don't take a donkey to the Kentucky Derby"
— **Pat Summit, head coach,
Tennessee Volunteers Women's Basketball**

It was probably my sixth Perfect Day, and Agents from out-of-town were visiting as observers. To ensure everything would indeed be perfect, I had met with my team members at midnight in the office.

That morning as my visitors were just settling in, one of my team members, Dave, came up to me and blurted out in front of everyone, "Oh God, I can't wait 'til this day is over."

He gave the wrong impression, and it just took the wind out of everyone's sails.

My other team members, who had been around for awhile, glanced up, each catching my eye with the same question on their lips:

"Do you want me to pack his stuff?"

I said, "No, I'll enjoy this."

And the next minute, I'm standing over his desk, packing his stuff.

In disbelieve, he was asking, "What are you doing?"

I cleared it out—the whole desk.

"I've got another person coming in soon," I told him.

He was gone.

You have to fire people.

It has to be quick.

If you are keeping a person, or you have doubts about a person, it is costing you at minimum $60,000 to $80,000 above his or her $40,000 salary. You are losing performance. It's like losing a total of $100,000 because you're just thinking about getting rid of them.

If you have even an inkling that a team member may not be working out for you, you must fire that person.

But you also have to really enjoy doing it. Seriously. If you can't find enjoyment, then hand this duty off to your Agency manager.

It may be that you take the chair that's at his desk. Just remove it, just take it away. When he comes in, asking: "Where's my chair?" It's gone.

Have fun with it.

I'm dead serious.

Training agents are going broke because they don't want to fire someone.

The new agent will insist, they'll swear, "Yeah, I could fire someone just like that!"

But after the interview, now that you're an Agent, you will be calling everyone:

"Um, Suzy, do you really think I should fire him?"

"Hello, Janet, do you think I should fire him?"

"Steve, should I fire him?"

And the only advice you will get from each and every one of them will be "Fire him!"

But you still haven't fired him.
You're wasting money.

Look at it this way: If some other Agent came into your office, walked up to that person and offered to double his or her pay, will that person stay with you?

Absolutely not.

It's business.

We are business owners. Business owners can't afford to make those types of mistakes.

Think about how your family will suffer from the stress of this situation if you don't correct it. Even if you run an Agency like a family, if you are friends with the people who work for you, your team members need to understand that your family always comes above them.

You're not supposed to be friends with the people in your Agency. You can be friendly. I know it's a small office, and you naturally can become friends. If it reaches that point, when a nonperforming team member is costing you money, you have to explain that your family comes first and your family will not suffer for any team member.

Part II

Creating the "A" Team Agency Draft

When I first started almost 10 years ago, I had a goal in mind.

First, I looked at what types of job functions I wanted to put in place.

If I hired "staff" first, I didn't think they were going to produce very much. So, instead of recruiting "staff," a term I find demeaning and never use to refer to any employees, I recruited potential Agents. And, surprisingly, I found myself in competition with my own Company's recruiting efforts for its intern programs.

At first, I would go to a college, and I would basically say, "Hey, do you want to be an agent with my Company?"

How many people in colleges want to be insurance agents? Not very many. College graduates hate cold calling and door-to-door sales. So it didn't work.

But how many people in college want to own their own business? All of them.

There's a different way that you have to recruit these individuals.

Hire Agents.

Hire people who are going to act like you and then give them more responsibility.

The more responsibility you give, the happier they'll be.

Isn't that the craziest thing?

The more power you give away, the more power you'll have.

I go to colleges to find my team members. The colleges have already tested for me.

When I first started as an agent, I looked at resumes. Today, I look at test scores.

In Dayton, Ohio, I hired at four levels:

- part-time high school students
- part-time college interns

- full-time college graduates
- part-time elderly people as receptionists

This creates a ladder that allows workers to move from high school, through local colleges and into the positions that can launch them into high-paying Agency positions or ownership.

Sometimes the interns outrun the graduates and are first to reach their goal of Agency and independence. But I attribute that to my system that encourages the full-time team members to hand off as much work as possible to the part-time students. The full-time team members are also responsible as mentors for the part-timers, assisting their subordinates to ascend the Agency's career ladder.

Pre-Interview Testing

I think it's best to hire someone to come to your Agency to evaluate your organizational style. These experts can prepare individualized tests for your Agency's prospective team members. This is one of the few areas where spending your cash really pays off.

For help in finding an agency, go to www.BigAlf.com for a list of agencies to choose from.

The Tryouts

The interviews of possible team members are always focused on the team member, not the Agent.

I never tell a prospective hire, "This is what I need you to do at this Agency."

That is just the start of a bad relationship.

1st Interview — Always With Me

I want to know if this person is competitive. Here's what I put on the table:

> **"If you work in my office, within two years, I'm going to give you the opportunity to own your own business."**

Some people I have hired have been able to leave before the two-year period, but that's what I tell them when they come in for the first time.

Having said that, I tell them right up front, they are not going to be paid very much. My pay is $12 an hour. I believe you can pay $12 an hour for this position in any state of the country. Any area where you find a McDonald's, you can pay $12 for your team members.

But again, they are getting an opportunity to become an Agent. I have never had an Agent who had fulfilled the two-year stint leave and make less than $100,000 in the first year.

When you look at those recruits coming into my office, what are they thinking?

"I've got to suffer for two years, and then what?"—"I'm getting paid."

Hire for attitude. Train for skill.

Next, I have job candidates interview me.

"You can ask any question you like," I'll say.

I'm looking for that one question about what is most important on their minds: Money.

When they ask, "How much do you make?"

I show my check.

2nd Interview — With My Team

My team interviews each candidate.

It may involve keeping a candidate in the office for half a day just to make sure the fit will be good.

I want my new hires to understand what the position is. I tell each of them, "You will be on the phone a lot."

3rd Interview — With the Management Office

New hires must meet the Management Office to understand that their job opportunities extend beyond just my office.

The Management Office may put you off, and offer excuses such as implying that these prospective hires aren't your employees yet.

Here's my response: "These people are potential Agents. I don't care if only the Management Office secretary is available; I want my new hire to meet with someone there.

What am I setting up here?

If this person truly wants to be an Agent and knows there will be only two years to get it done, the realization strikes immediately: "I need to put up some numbers."

Who is going to make that decision to promote to an Agency? Not me. It's the Management Office. So when the Management Office comes in to see who's ready for a promotion, my team member will make the first impression.

4th Interview – Optional With Top Clients

Recently, I have offered to my top 100 clients the opportunity to participate in the interview process for new hires. I've found this establishes closer client relationships with the Agency.

Welcome Packet

When I've made my decision to hire someone, I send out a Welcome Packet.

The Welcome Packet includes

- my handbook
- employment documents
- five books that I require them to read before Flight School
- a procedures manual. I call mine "Play Book."
- a blank DVD, representing the Flight Book. On the DVD is written: "How good do you want to become?"

Again, I want this person to understand more than just the responsibilities of the job that will be the first step of the career ladder. I want new team members to understand the entire Agency and what everyone does. I want new hires to appreciate that I am serious about training them to be team members and Agents, not "staff."

Motivation

I can't motivate team members, but I hope to inspire them.

Do you think these Agents-in-training are going to run hard from the first day they arrive?

Let's examine this from a different angle. I see Agents make mistakes by looking for salespeople. They believe new employees are tough to identify, and they think: "I've got to find a salesperson. I've got to find someone who can sell. I need a professional."

My question is: "What is the professional salesperson going to do?"

Here's what the typical new Agent will answer: "Well I've got this service person—they're going to service. And my salesperson is going to sell."

The more team members you have as a new Agent, the tougher it is. I'm not saying not to have them, but it's just tougher because you're doing more management than you are doing anything else.

If you have more team members, more planning is required of you. They need to know their role, their place, their mission and their assignment. Your job is to delegate. Place them in charge of something. It can be putting the team's numbers on a board or organizing messages left on the phones. They should be charged with preparing and presenting weekly reports on their areas of specialization at the team meetings.

Your new team member doesn't know what to do on the first day of work. As the Agent, you may end up with three people just staring at each other. And you're paying them. It's especially tough when payday comes and you see those team members just sitting there. Don't that hurt? You're like, "What are they doing here?"

One of my good friends, an Agent, once observed: "I had three team members, and I'm down to one. The crazy thing is that with only one, production is higher than with three."

Think of all that money she paid for those three team members when she only needed to pay for one. That hurts.

She was not managing her team members correctly. It happens in a lot of Agencies. When there are too many people and they are not managed, most of them just sit around with nothing to do.

When you hire that new person for your team, you must tell explain and demonstrate: "Here's what we did without you. Three months from now, if it still looks like that, we are going to be without you again."

Training

After the hire and the first day of orientation, the next thing we think about is, "Just get this person licensed, and we're ready to go!"

What's missing?

Training.

I had the greatest feeling of accomplishment when first I realized my system was working. It happened during a call from an Agent in New York to Andy Lewis, who was then one of my team members.

The Agent said, "Andy, I've got 20 staff people. You guys have three. How in the world are you writing more fire apps than us?"

Andy said, "We don't have any staff people in here. We just have Agents."

Train them as Agents.

How many business plans are approved in this country, and yet, they don't include training? Training is the most important part of any business plan.

But how many Agencies have a training program?

Most Agents just assume, "Oh, they'll learn as they go."

These Agents want to hold their team members accountable, especially for any shortcomings. But they don't train.

Does that make sense?

And then these Agents spend money on top of that. In the first three months, an Agent may spend, $20,000 to $40,000 on other things and yet still have untrained team members answering the phones.

Before these new Agents know it, they're in debt.

When they look around to find the problem, they'll say, "The marketing didn't really work."

But the marketing worked. The marketing is team members answering the phone. Those team members may have taken about six months to train themselves, but they finally got trained—off your marketing dollars.

For example, a potential customer calls the Agency for an appointment. But on the other end, they hear: "Hold on. I'm doing a vehicle change."

Does that make sense? Yet this is what goes on when there is no training.

A variation of this type of catastrophe happens when the people who have received training for a specific position aren't trained to know what Agency really is about. So a person, trained only in service, goes in and fixes service.

"Shoot, I did a great job. I'm servicing all your customers," is what you'll hear from them. But did those team members pivot once? No, but they kept busy.

Put new hires through a training process in your office. Be certain they learn everything about Agency and their positions.

Your training should be very basic. The kids coming out of colleges and high schools don't know what we mean by "customer service." All their lives, they've had 1-800 numbers and spent their time talking to someone in India—I don't know where. But that's what they think customer service is. "I'm sorry sir, but I'm on the other side of the world. You will have to fix your smart phone."

It's amazing.

You know how some businesses' customer services put you on hold, or cut you off, or leave you listening to music that hurts your ears? You can't have that in your office; you've got to teach this stuff.

So what's the difference?

My System. I call it "Flight School."

Flight School

After you've found the right people to work for you, you must build the office culture.

It starts with a Vision Board.

If you are not familiar with the concept, it's a way of acting out and organizing your dreams, goals and ambitions.

A Vision Board can be constructed by pasting up cut-outs from magazines on a piece of cardboard. Encourage this person to find the house they ultimately want to live in, the car they want to drive, and the kind of people they want to have as friends and lovers.

There is also software that allows you to cull photographs from a variety of popular magazines to create a virtual Vision Board as a screen saver for a computer.

This tells you a lot about the people you have hired; and it serves to motivate them because it broadcasts those dreams to everyone in the office without saying a word around the water cooler.

I link the Vision Board with a mandatory visit to my Company's employee assistance program, which offers psychological and financial counseling.

I look for the best people, but some of them have arrived with some pretty heavy "baggage." There are those who have minor personality issues, a few have relationship issues and some may have alcohol or drug dependency issues that must be resolved. There may be credit debts and other loans that piled up. I've hired people with Attention Deficit Disorder who needed further counseling to assist them in focusing on the matters at hand.

Employee Assistance Programs

You paid for it, you should use it. I've never met a perfect person. I tell each new hire:

> **"You will go to our Employee Assistance Program and sit down with a counselor at least one time."**

Employee Assistance Programs help your team members with alcohol abuse, divorce, financial binds and personal relationships.

Some new team members will have bad credit. Some, even the young hires, may have an alcohol problem. The counselor will help find a way out of that situation. Again, these new team members are motivated to work with the counselor because they know it's just a hurdle on the way to Agency.

The new hire sits down and talks with a counselor. If nothing else, the counselor reviews the employee's financial situation and puts them in a psychological and financial position that readies each of them for Agency when the time comes.

Next comes the training:

I. Customer Service (one day)
    a. Learning phone etiquette
        i. Greeting
        ii. Placing on hold
    b. Being proactive
        i. Using OHIO—"Only Handle It Once"
        ii. Giving full explanations of procedures
        iii. Ensuring that customers understand
        iv. Reviewing frequently asked questions
    c. Handling complaints
        i. Videotaping practices of participants
        ii. Using Feel, Felt, Found

II. Presenting Coverages (2 days)
    a. Explaining in "Baby Terms"
    b. Creating consistent experiences —>Referrals

III. Quoting (2 days)

        a.   Developing speed in preparation & presentation
        b.   Teaching customers over the phone
        c.   Multi-Lining

IV.   Practicing with Real Customers while being monitored and critiqued (five days)

Flight School focuses on teaching new team members about the most important areas that can immediately create income for your Agency.

By gaining skills in these three areas, customer service, presentation of coverages and quoting, your new team member will be producing income within a month.

Community Service

Each of my team members contributes one hour of community service each month. They may be assisting at a food shelter or a local school.

In Dayton, our most successful program was to participate in a Company-sponsored event jointly held with the National Urban League.

Called Read & Rise, it is an NUL program to foster scholastic achievement among African American students.

Our office contributed half-days for three months to organize and coordinate with the local chapter of the Urban League. We were involved in finding other sponsors for the events and reserving the venue, a new theater that was built at the center of the city. This event, with tickets selling for as much as $300, sold out.

During that event, there was time set aside when I was able to sit with Maya Angelou and Oprah Winfrey, two of the participants. They basically explained to me about being a hero and leaving a legacy. They appreciated my accomplishments. During the program, I was recognized for my participation. But they really sat me down and said "You've done a great job, but take it to another level where it can do things across the country." And it has.

If you look at my former team members, they have Agencies across the country, and they are doing the same things.

In subsequent years, we brought Wall Street banker Raymond J. McGuire and former Secretary of State Colin Powell as speakers for the event.

All of this stems from a team meeting we held at my Agency when three things came together:

1. *The Magic of Thinking Big*. In that meeting, that book made us think big. Who else would think about bringing Oprah and Maya together?

2. We always were big on community service at our Agency.

3. Empowering the team members. They came up with the ideas. It wasn't just my idea.

Our Agency was noticed and praised by these two icons. This transformed our insurance Agency into something that's bigger than just an insurance Agency, and I think that's what all companies ultimately try to achieve, usually through their philanthropy.

I felt that we, my team members and I, reached our vision of what we wanted this Agency to be.

Implementing AL's Systems

We've come a long way to get to this point in the book.

It may seem overwhelming to consider trying to implement my systems with a team that you have already put into place using conventional insurance agency models.

No one expects you to bring a game clock into the office tomorrow and try to start up a Perfect Day with a staff whose morale may already be sagging and whose methods are haphazard or just out-of-sync.

The son of a top-50 Agent spent time in my office not too long ago. Here's a summary of what he found:

> *Far more effective than making changes on the margin, system creation has the power to revolutionize an insurance agency. A system allows each component of an agency to add up to far more than just the sum of its parts, a fact that is nowhere more present than in AL Sicard's Insurance Agency. His system, in its simplicity, generates the most outcome with very little resources compared to the average agency. This model system, which places emphasis on his*

team members, maximizes lead generation, lead conversion, and retention rate to get the most out of investment.

– Dave Munson Jr.

I've found the way to implement these systems requires that you involve your entire team from the beginning.

There are three important steps to get from where you are to where I am:

- Create a Business Plan
- Set aside two weeks for training in a Retreat Setting
- Establish a 90-day probation period

The Business Plan
Where Are We Now?

In developing a business plan, each member of your team must be on the same page as you. Everyone should agree about goals for the new systems that will be put in place. These goals must be measurable.

The goals must come from the team members, not you, the Agent. You can't give someone goals and expect them to be accepted. The key is to have each of your team members develop the goals they believe are necessary to make the Agency successful.

Here are examples of appropriate goals:

- Develop plans to win a specific award that your Company offers.
- Measure the current customer retention rate then set a higher mark for after implementing my systems.
- Tabulate the number of referrals you are getting now then count the referrals after my systems have had time to be established.
- Photograph the office, its walls, doors and desks. Set a date after the new systems are in place when you will take more photographs for comparison.

- Document your current office procedures along with any specific variances that depend on who performed them. Use this documentation later to track whether the performance of procedures is more uniform after the systems are in place.

The Retreat

Start your plans for a retreat by giving your team members a reading assignment such as reading my Flight Kit books. Have each member write a couple of paragraphs about each book.

A retreat should be at a nice facility. Hotels in a campground or a park setting offer a good atmosphere for a retreat. I hold my retreats at Aileron, Clay Mathile's institution just north of Dayton. It's a beautiful, relaxing campus. Team members immediately grasp the concept that this will not be another day or week in the office and that something important is about to happen.

Some Agents I know have taken their teams to Las Vegas. I like Las Vegas, but I don't think it's a good place for a retreat. There are just too many distractions. I think retreats should be in secluded areas.

While your team is at the retreat, you don't have to close the Agency. Have another Agent send over one or two team members to handle phone calls or emergencies while your team is focused on implementing my systems. If you have part-time team members, you may consider leaving them in charge.

At the retreat, let the team members lead the discussions. Work through my systems by having team members take responsibility for the implementation of specific systems and the measurement of progress toward the goals.

Assignments can be

- organizing the desks to ensure they are identical
- charting progress on pivots and phone calls
- preparing the scheduling board and assigning the colors
- recording the changes as they happen and as they become ingrained in the team members' work habits

Plan to bring out the cameras and photograph the desks, walls and the people in the office. Are their vision boards in sight? What does it look like a week after the retreat? A month after the retreat? Three months after the retreat?

The 90-Day Probation Period

During the week after the retreat, there should be immediate follow-up with each individual. As the Agent, you must begin to evaluate all team members about where they are in the process of implementing each of the systems.

Are their desks cleared of everything but the one thing they are working on? Are four folders on each desk? Are they remembering to document everything?

After this initial evaluation period, begin to assign these tasks to individual team members. Let them do the tracking for you. Remember, the ultimate goal is to remove you, the Agent, from the entire process.

Start up the team meetings as soon as you return from the retreat. It must be emphasized in the most serious terms that team meetings require the attendance of everyone—even if there is a customer in the office. Grant no excuses for missing team meetings. Team members may have to learn to schedule their appointments around team meetings.

Implementing AL's Systems: A Neighborly Approach

In 2009, another Agent in town recognized the success I had achieved and asked me about trying out some of my systems. He is a good Agent, who opened his Agency about when I started mine. But he wanted to take it to another level.

We arranged for his newest hire, Chris Weaver, to be the go-between for our Agencies. Chris was a recent university graduate who had majored in education. He had planned to teach, but he applied for a job with the other insurance Agency to help pay his bills. Substitute teaching did not pay benefits. Work at the Agency was steady compared to the subbing jobs he had been taking after graduation.

I met Chris about two weeks after he was hired. He visits my office once a month, meeting with my team members, taking notes and observing my systems.

Here's what Chris had to say about the past year:

By no means did I grow up thinking I wanted to be in insurance. But that's all I'm looking at now.

When I started, there were just two of us team members and our Agent who also was there 9 to 5 doing the exact same things that we were doing.

I was watching a college basketball game the other day. The analyst was explaining how sometimes a young team, or a team that doesn't really know what it's doing, can be good because its members have a belief that they can win—they don't know they can win, but they think they can—and then they transition to greatness once they do beat the really good opponent. Or they have that one signature win, so they know they can do it.

I liken that to my boss's office, where he thought he could do really good, but he just didn't really know how.

But once we took some of the systems in AL's office and started implementing them in ours, we were able to have our first month with over 100 apps. We also completed one of the two-month Life promotions this past year, too. And then the whole mindset changes from "We think we can do this" to "We know we can."

Now it's "We need to do this every time." And if we don't have over 100 apps every month, he's not going to be happy.

Chris found a lot of material at AL's to bring back to his boss and team members.

AL's really good at painting that picture. You know, "What do you want?" and "Here's how you can get it."

The whole "working smarter, not harder thing." It seems most great ideas are pretty simple ideas. A lot of systems that we took from AL are simple, in hindsight—yet, we didn't think of them. And he did think of them.

Chris found my systems easy to use.

They weren't hard to implement. We had to tweak them for our office.

It started with the training. When I started, my boss did not have any set training at all for me. But when I came over to AL's office, one of his team members likened his orientation to "boot camp," where the first couple weeks involved reading books to get an understanding of how to make yourself better. And you have to make a vision board. Now we do those as well. I think that strengthens the bond between the team members and Agent. There is a feeling that if they are helping the Agent out, the Agent is going to help them out as well—to make their dreams and meet their goals in life.

We implemented the video taping as well to help us refine the way we talk to people and to use the "Baby Terms" when explaining coverages and to show how a successful Life appointment should go.

We also are trying to get that "Wow!" experience, to make a customer "Wowed" and to have an amazing experience in the office. We're still working on that. It doesn't really just boil down to price. They want to stay because of the treatment they got at that office.

And then there is the follow-up with the customers. There're just so many things that have really helped out a lot.

One of the things that AL said that really stuck was "Eagles don't fly in flocks." If you see everybody doing something one way and it's not working for them, why not go off in the other direction and try that out?

We see a lot of Agents struggling, and the visions that they had are not turning out for them, yet they refuse to try something different. I don't know if it's because they are scared or they just don't know how, yet.

Chris said his boss has been very supportive of his efforts as liaison between the two offices. But Chris sees now that change first must come from the team members.

I think the best way to get an Agent to do something is to have the team on board. I think my boss realizes that. I think having a team member come back and go: "Wow. They get twice as much done over there, twice as easy, and this is how they're doing it."

The first person I talk to is actually the other team member in the office. So we're both on board with the idea, and the only person we have to convince is the Agent. If we're both on board, and we're showing him: "Hey, this is going to improve your numbers and make your Agency better, and at the same time make our jobs easier and make the customers happier and everything else. It's a win-win for everybody."

The other Agent hired four interns, two from high school and two in college to assist Chris and the other licensed team member in the office.

The interns kind of shield us from a lot of the service aspects. Making copies, a lot of the paper work. They also provide us with a lot of leads so we can call people back and close sales.

Chris found that changes that worked spurred everyone in his office.

It gets everyone pumped. After we implemented the systems, most people don't really like change, or it's just hard for them to do it. But once we did it, I mean, it was an immediate result.

We started implementing AL's systems in March 2009. And in one month—there was a kind of learning curve in there—and by May, we did over 100 apps. And somehow or another, we did about 30 or more Life apps.

And everybody's spirits just raised, too. The other Agent and I are happy because we're just selling and dealing with people about things that they actually need for them, rather than handling all the service and stuff. My boss is happier because his Agency is booming. The sky's the limit for him now. Next year, he's got some amazing goals that he wants to achieve.

Like the team members in my office, Chris draws his motivation from his new goal: to become an Agent with his own business. After that realization, he said he's been working harder than ever.

You're not just going to be handed that. You have to work hard. And obviously, coming from a successful Agency helps tremendously because then you can show them: "This is what I've already done. This is what I'm going to do with my own Agency."

Chris wasn't just the water carrier for the other Agent, he's learned valuable lessons that he will build upon when he opens his own Agency:

I would surround myself with successful people. If I'm starting a new Agency, I want to hire team members that have that same drive that I do—that have dreams about a bigger and better life. Because I don't want somebody coming in that wants to stay either. They'll just get complacent. I want somebody who wants to get their own Agency because then they are going to work for that.

I think I would tweak the vision board and have them write out some of their dreams, too. That's the beauty of these systems. You can always be tweaking them, and you always should be.

Date Night: Don't Forget Your Family

With my systems in place, I've done my best to get you, the new Agent, out of the business. But the time you gain from using these systems must not be squandered.

Recall my earlier remarks about how so many Agents have found themselves in the New Agent Graveyard. But there are no joint burial plots there. No His and Hers grave stones. By the time Agents reach the gates of NAG, most Agents' marriages are in shambles.

This business creates excessive stress on families. Agents become enamored with their new business. Every conversation with a spouse or loved one begins, "The agency this . . . " or "The agency that . . ." These Agents are stressed out, and their spouses have no idea how to support them because the spouses have no idea about what's going on back at the Agency.

The Agents have told their spouses about how they were going to make very specific, large amounts of money in their endeavor, but when the money fails to come in at the rate they anticipated, that's when the weak links in a marriage begin to snap.

Sometimes the marriage disintegrates while the Agent is away on a business seminar, staying in a hotel with other frustrated and stressed agents. And those stressed out people often find each other, and then there is a real mess to deal with.

In the average class of 25 new Agents, maybe a couple will do well. The bulk will struggle as they search for some model that will bring them their dream. A lot of Agents never figure it out.

I believe your spouse needs to understand your business. Your spouse must be involved in the business in some way, even if it is just acting as a "secret shopper" to measure the quality of your customer service.

If you implement my plan, you will have much less stress at home. You won't have to continually second-guess your team members. They will be fine without you.

Your family, on the other hand, will never be fine without you.

To cope with all of this, I will offer you one more system: Date Night.

You need to set aside at least one night a week when it's just you and your spouse—together and away from everyone else.

And if you have little ones, they will need special time, too. After all, they are the ones who this was all supposed to be about.

Part III

Player Haters

Success brings its own rewards, it's said. But success also brings some nasty issues that you will have to learn to live with.

Maya Angelou has written so much about those who envy successful people. Oprah often speaks about how she has had to struggle with these issues.

And, as Wall Street banker Raymond J. McGuire likes to say,

"Eagles do not fly in flocks."

So just expect that some people, even some other agents, may be throwing rocks at you instead of applauding your good fortune.

Some may be saying that you are abusing the system to make your fortune. I like to believe that they do this not because they dislike me, but because they are so frustrated with their own foundering business that they must believe that a successful person in the same business is just cheating. It's not just this business, but I think you will find that anywhere in our society.

If unfounded charges are brought against you, it will be your Company's obligation to investigate. And you should welcome it. Be prepared for it, and when it happens, open your doors with an expectant smile.

Relish it, because it will be your opportunity to show the Company how well your Agency is performing.

Of course, this means, if you are striving for the top, you cannot afford to cut corners. No one cares if the guy at the far end of the bench is using steroids—but if the team's star once sought out pharmaceutical enhancers—goodbye reputation. Everyone is watching.

Your team members must understand this, too. It will become a sense of pride in your office that each of you is part of a model agency.

Your Company's Management

Memo to New Agents:

Although you will have your own business, during the first year, you will have a manager or management team. They will sometimes insist that you do things their way and not the way you would like to do things.

Many times you will be asked to spend more on the Company's marketing materials and to hire more team members.

Even if you think you are being misled, my advice is to swim with the current, not against it. Being obstinate with your management team can be frustrating and very stressful. It's important that you accept their directions and advice. Later, you can make adjustments.

What I have seen during nearly a decade in this business is that management usually is correct and offers reasonable advice. You must keep in mind that as a new, and maybe a young Agent, you don't yet fully comprehend the business, but you will believe you are smarter than they are.

I found the best Agents in the Company have good relationships with the management office and rely on its advice. I've always used my management office. My Company's managers have been my best friends.

One of the frequent complaints I hear is: "My consultants tell me to do it this way, and I'm not allowed to do it my way."

If you are in your first year, you are trying to gain control of the job, so you always do what "They" say. They have a better view of the business than you. Once you've learned the business and done it "Their" way, you can always do it your way.

I have found that, if the Agent explains up front to the managers what the business plan entails and how the Agent wants to run the business, "They" will support you on that as long as you are successful in implementing these types of systems. However, if you are not successful, the game is over.

You need to listen to your consultants because, obviously, they didn't get to that position without being successful.

When I was a trainee Agent, I was a leader in Home and Auto insurance.

An ego comes with that, and with that ego, I thought I could do no wrong. My consultant comes in one day and basically says, "Hey! You're terrible at Life insurance."

At that point, I wasn't a person who wanted to hear that I was terrible at anything while I'm leading in two lines of insurance. The consultant angered me so much that it hurt our relationship.

Years later, I realized that if she had not had that conversation with me, I probably would have lost more than $500,000.

Today, I can say that the people who are the toughest with you are the people who care the most about you.

If my consultant had come in and said, "You're the greatest with Auto and Fire," I would have lost $500,000 in my career.

I take pride in the fact that any Agents who came from my Agency do not have problems with Management. That's because, if they do have problems with Management, and I hear about it, there's going to be a conversation that is not going to be much fun.

Basically, I love my Company, and the way to keep my Company strong is to ensure that everybody has open communications and is cooperative.

Right in my business plan, it says:

"For my Company to be profitable, well-managed, growth oriented and to have communication credibility."

I think that should be in every Agent's business plan and that you should hold yourself accountable for that.

I allow my Management Office to conduct an internal and external audit. They basically conduct a systems check to ensure that I am working my plan.

I offer this final observation:

I have seen very few Agents who did not believe in the Company—who were not on the same page as the Company—make a lot of money.

Part IV

Stories of Success

Up to this point, I've outlined the systems a new Agent needs to obtain a functioning business that will be able to run itself. And I've tried to justify why these systems are so crucial to have in place as you begin on the road to success and steer clear of the New Agent Graveyard.

Next, I offer you a glimpse of what other Agents see in this business. You don't have to read about all of them. My intention is to offer you a wide range of Agents' personal views and experiences so that you may find one or two, maybe more, who resonate with you.

I've included accounts from Agents who started fresh out of college, such as **Jackie Padesky**, **Andy Lewis**, **Anh Nguyen** and **Devan DeClue**.

Jackie walked into my Agency and everything just clicked. At first, she was reluctant about Sales, but she saw that selling was a way of helping people. And helping people is the motivating force in her life. But she also had dreams of ownership and maintaining ties to her family.

Andy is one of the most driven individuals I have ever met. A devoted, young father, he was hell-bent on grasping an opportunity to own his own business while he drove my business to the top of the charts. He stumbled, but he had the fortitude and presence of mind to get right back up and win his seat back in the blink of an eye.

Anh worked for an agency while finishing her college studies, then entered her Company's Agent training program after graduation. She chose me to mentor her as she prepared to open her Agency, and since then she has installed several of my systems, some modified by her and her team members.

Devan was working as a cocktail waitress and event planner while finishing her undergraduate studies at Ohio State University. She quickly realized the opportunity Agency could offer her. Stepping into my office, she gained confidence as a public speaker and found a way to realize her dreams and those of her parents. She recently moved to California where she is awaiting an opening for her first Agency.

Several of these stories come from incredibly gifted athletes and performers whose experiences at the highest level of sports or performing arts gave them skills to develop team relationships and leadership skills necessary to establish themselves as the C.E.O.s of their businesses.

Greg Orton, who worked part-time in my Agency while he was in high school and later during breaks from Purdue University, has NFL agents eying him while he contemplates his own Agency on the side. He credits his public speaking skills to experiences with telemarketing from my office.

Look at the threesome of **Ben Raymond**, **Travis Trice** and **Cynthia Brown**, all gifted, athletic performers, who gained experience in other industries before entering the field occupied by tens of thousands of insurance agents in this country.

Ben and Travis were college basketball players and relied on their natural friendliness to propel them to their goals as successful agents.

Ben, whose wife works in a different state and is a professional basketball player, found his calling by developing new Agents at his Agency in Texas at a lightning-fast pace. Ben hustled through his training programs and was a quick study in developing his playbook while making after-hours visits to my Agency.

Travis and his wife are raising five wonderful and gifted children, attending all of their kids' activities. They achieved this while Travis holds the additional responsibilities of being a head basketball coach at a large high school with a highly competitive team that includes his eldest son.

Cynthia, a modern and classical dancer, walked away from a successful career in finance as a C.P.A. in Atlanta, to take up an Agency near her hometown of Washington, D.C., where she is able to find more time to tend to her other interests: supporting a dance company with the cause of tending to the healing of abused women.

Finally, **Deseral Neal** demonstrates that a single Mom with two children can have it all. Starting as a mail clerk, Deseral worked full time in a regional office while raising her kids at the kitchen table where they all studied their assignments. After earning a bachelors degree and then an M.B.A., Deseral jumped right into Agency training and opened her new office in the most congested part of a heavily urbanized, New Jersey city that opened its arms in gratitude to her.

Jackie Padesky

Jackie was at AL's Agency from November 2005 to May 2008.

In May 2009, Jackie Padesky was granted an Agency in Lacon, Ill., a town of less than 2,000 residents located 24 miles north of Peoria and 108 miles south of Chicago. The Agency's previous owner died tragically in a car accident. Jackie, 26, had been an intern Agent assigned to the region for one year.

Born and raised in central Illinois, Jackie is the daughter of a life-long worker for one of the state's largest corporations that makes earth-moving equipment. Jackie wanted to emulate her hard-working parents' envious lifestyle but on her own terms.

Jackie's first job after college was as a service person in the auto division of a large insurance company's regional office. She sat in a cubicle, assisting agents or team members who called with questions about applications they were sending in for auto insurance.

Four months into her job, Jackie's new husband, Greg, entered a graduate program at the University of Dayton in Ohio to study theology, with the goal of becoming a campus minister. The young couple's focus on community service is immediately apparent: they met at a Habitat for Humanity project while at Southern Illinois University Carbondale.

In Dayton, Jackie immediately sought a job in insurance with the same Company. She came across AL's Agency and was drawn to his approach to the business and his efforts at community service.

I think we connected more on a level about our philanthropic work. I was very passionate about community service, and I knew he was as well.

Being new to the area, I was excited to be involved with somebody who I could see had a passion for that as well and was as actively involved and trying to do things. And I knew that that would be a great way for me to become more familiar with the area. That was what got me originally so excited about the area. And the fact that I was going to be able to represent the same Company. It was kind of the best of both worlds for me.

I was in the right place at the right time. And, boy, do I know that now.

I had earned a marketing degree, and I knew that Sales would be something I would probably get into down the road. At my first job, Sales was not much of an issue because I was talking about products with people who sold those products. There wasn't a real level of pressure right there.

Stepping into AL's office was kind of forcing me into something that was new.

What really sold me about AL, besides his involvement in the community and the great things he was doing, he approached the Sales role in a different way. He always told me, "We don't sell to the customers, the customers buy from us."

We had the benefit of knowing our Company was the best company in the world, and because of that, our products and services were really highly regarded. So we weren't trying to sell so much the idea of our Company as being the right company, but it was more trying to match the right product to the right person.

Very early on, AL changed my mind about what Sales is. It isn't pushing something at somebody or trying to talk them into something. It is just helping them find the right thing for them because everybody has one need or another.

And that was huge for me. That was instrumental in changing my idea about what Sales is and about how I could approach Agency as a career. It wasn't scary then. It became a challenge.

AL challenged her at every step.

Jackie received her licensing and prepared to start at AL's agency with a title "Sales Associate."

It was a period when AL's other team members were departing—only one remained. For a few months, she was the only team member in the office.

So, at that point, you might say, I kind of stepped into the office manager role.

It was almost a hot seat approach: Here's what you do. Learn it as you go. And you become very quick at it.

AL sat me down and said, "Here's how you're going to learn Auto."

And he handed me the phone, and then there was a live customer, and AL said, "Okay. Go.'"

At the time, I would get very red and very nervous. I wouldn't speak nervous. I wouldn't act nervous. But, if you looked at me, I'd be blotchy. I'd be broken out and just so nervous because I was on the spot.

Through the video taping and through the practice role playing and through the interactions and other stuff like that, he helped me get over that very quickly. It really helped me in the long run because now I know how to handle that kind of stress, and I can get through with no problem.

So, very early on he got me to get over some of my fears, just by forcing me to be in the hot seat and to be video-taped and role-played and put on the spot to talk about things we were doing and things like that. It was great.

I can't say enough about AL's systems and about how smart he is and how he runs his Agency. I know he strives to have his Agency run like a McDonald's.

Although I haven't had as long a time to set up my Agency that well and to have my systems that strongly in place, that's a goal of mine and something that we're striving to get to.

It's really fun. I've learned so much from him. More than anything, I've learned how to be a student of the business. To continually challenge myself. And to continually try to learn about the business that I'm working in.

After the first six months or so, AL started talking to me about the idea of Agency and about how Agency could afford me all the things I valued in life. How I could give back to the community and be successful and be independent and own my own business.

I think he was smart in how he developed me. He really built my confidence. He made me see that I could dream big and showed me how to achieve it. Not just how to dream big, but how to break down the dream into possible steps to get you there.

All of the things he knew now that I valued, he was able to present that to me with the idea of Agency and what that could do for me. And that took on a whole other level of understanding of what my position was in his office. I saw it as an opportunity to make myself better; to learn by having him as a mentor 24/7; to show me how to prepare myself for success.

So the last year-and-a- half or two years that I was there, it was really just me trying to be a sponge and absorb everything that I could from him.

We did vision boards very early on. Right about the time that we sat down and started talking about trying to reach some of the bigger goals within our Company: top in the nation in Fire and stuff like that. When we sat down, that was kind of our vision board planning session.

We had a new team member at the time, Andy Lewis. At that point, it was Andy, Heather and I in the office. Plus there was some intern help here and there from some high schoolers. But for the most part, it was just the three of us.

When we sat down, it was kind of "What do we all want to do individually? How can our work in the Agency help us with our individual goals? How can some of the goals within the Agency help us with our individual goals and how can we help the Agency?" It kind of all worked itself out to where one benefited the other.

And those vision boards were so critical to that because it kind of kept us on point then—as to why we were doing what we were doing. Because of course there are those days where you struggle, and there're days when you are in a bad mood or you don't necessarily want to be there. But knowing what the greater purpose of it was, those vision boards really helped to put that front and center, to keep that in our minds.

I actually implemented the vision boards here in Lacon not too long ago with the girls in my office. About a month or two ago—we had been together just a few months—and I decided maybe it would help us to get to know each other a little better and maybe help us define why we got out of bed every morning and why we chose to come to my Agency every morning. You know, in terms of what our visions are for our futures, for our families, for our successes.

So we sat down and did a vision board activity just like we did in AL's office. And it was amazing what I got to learn about my team members. And what I think they got to learn about me, as well. So, I'm still using AL's ideas.

Jackie keeps her vision board by her desk.

Let me pull it out. I've got it right here. It's a big poster board. Let's see here. What's on my vision board? AL will laugh about this: part of my vision board, still, is I've always wanted to own a classic car.

AL always said that some day I would be the Agent that has all of the cars like socked away in some old barn that nobody knows about. So, I would love to have a '32 Ford Roadster. I would love to have a barn full of old cars. My husband and I have both committed to working really hard to solidify our careers early. At this point, we don't have any kids, but we hope to have a family soon. We have two dogs, Bonnie and Clyde. They're our kids.

So, things like that. I want to be able to travel. To have the time and be able to afford the things to be able to support my family and my friends and do all of the things that I love.

AL always says that I'm like a 65-year-old woman in a 26-year-old body because I love to crochet, and quilt and do some of the old-time crafty things. And Agency provides me the time to be able to do that when it's my time. You know, and my stress release.

I'm a huge motorcycle fan. My husband and I, in our families, kind of grew up around motorcycles. To be able to do those activities with our families, to go camping, and all of that is on my vision board. Having a garden is on there, and all of the little things that I care about. Agency allows me to do that because I've got the time and money to do it.

It's amazing.

I feel like I got front row, center seats to new Agency training when I was working with AL. I think he's the best in the world at it. I think he's got a great model. And he's so relatable.

I think the thing that is so impressive about AL is he's so larger than life. He comes across as such a character, but when you really get to know him, it's not all fluff. I mean he is 100 percent genuine—believes in what he does; loves what he does. Loves that he can afford other people the opportunity for the great career and the great lifestyle that he's earned. And I think that's so inspiring about him. He can give back so much to people by just doing what he loves to do.

It was a fun ride. Sometimes I look back and I think it was kind of unbelievable, but it really did happen. And I owe him for a lot of it. Almost all of it.

ANDY LEWIS

Andy Lewis worked at AL's Agency from August 2006 to August 2008. Andy spent six months in Agency training before he was granted an Agency in Washington Court House, Ohio, a city of about 13,000 people located half-way between the cities of Columbus and Cincinnati. At the age of 26, Andy signed his Agency contract in June 2009.

Born in Louisiana and raised by his parents in Xenia, Ohio, Andy was a high school athlete, participating in wrestling and soccer. Andy's father ran and operated his own business, a heavy paint manufacturing company. His Mom is a long time employee for the Xenia board of Education.

Andy attended Bowling Green State University for three years before transferring to Wright State University which is located near his hometown. He graduated in 2006 with a degree in business management and marketing. During his college years, Andy worked several internships in other types of businesses, including one with G.E. Nuclear Energy in North Carolina. But having heard about AL's Agency through a friend who had worked for AL, Andy asked her for an introduction shortly after he graduated.

I've always, always had aspirations to own my own business. I would have run through a brick wall, if, on the other side of that brick wall, was a business of my own.

In college, I wrote business plans for owning my own business. Never did I think I would do it when I was 26 years old. And I didn't know I would end up in insurance or on the financial side of things.

To get the job, I think I went in for three days in a row and just talked it up with AL. We talked about the opportunity, what he's been through, and I just fell in love with the idea of becoming a part of a large corporate insurance family.

We would be sitting there, and he would just call an agent on the phone and say, "Tell me about your life. Tell me how great your life is and how much you love your job." He let me talk to agents from around the country.

I think the interview process took a couple weeks. I was being interviewed when I didn't even know it. I found that out later.

I didn't care about the money that he was going to pay me. I didn't care about any of that. AL could give me the opportunities to one day own my own business, and that is all that mattered.

I'd never been in a hardcore Sales environment. I had been more on the business management side of it. But I've always known that I could talk to anybody. I feel like I can talk to anybody, and I think that's a quality that a lot of new agents and people in our positions have.

I was his Fire Guy. When I first got there, they were close to being in the top 100 in the country in Fire insurance. He introduced me to a couple of the apartment complexes. He had me get my license. Then he said, "We're at about 117 in the country right now in Fire. I would like to end up in the top 50."

I think we ended up right around 16th in the nation by the end of the year. And AL made it very clear that he wanted to be Number One in the country, although neither one of us had a precise idea of how to achieve that goal.

I got extremely involved with the apartment complexes and Fire, and that's how the whole ball got rolling to being Number One in Fire the next year. In January 2007, I built a business plan structured so that we would be adding more apartment complexes to our book of business so that we could sell renters insurance to their tenants.

Taking the first step of the plan, I went to the local grocery store and got a copy of the rental complex guide that holds hundreds of pages of lists of rental properties in the area. I called each rental complex and asked if they required renter's insurance. Those were the complexes I focused on. A large reason we were so successful in Fire was we had great relationships with our apartment complexes. I would visit the apartment complexes on a regular basis, either taking them lunch or just stopping by to chat. We ended up building very close and personal relationships with the staff members.

Our plan was to make a heavy push in the first six months of the year, but we didn't know three or four other Agencies across the country had the same idea. So we didn't break into the top five agencies until after mid-year.

Throughout all of this, I had shared custody of my 3-year-old son, child support payments and an apartment of my own to care for him. Obviously, the job with AL wasn't providing enough for us, so I had to find other jobs to support us. My personal problem was that my job with AL had irregular hours. I never knew if I'd be home at 6 o'clock or 10 o'clock as we pursued the grueling quotas that we needed.

My solution was to take jobs that wouldn't conflict with my job at AL's: bartending and catering at weekend weddings while I also was working security from 10 p.m. to 3 a.m. on Thursdays, Fridays and Saturdays at local night clubs or bars.

We were close to sleeping in the Agency office at times, just trying to get some numbers going. It's extremely, extremely stressful. But, on the other end of that, when it's going good, it's probably one of the best feelings you can ever have.

At times, some of the numbers AL would come up with and his approach to me were overwhelming. I was like, "There's just no way I can do this. There is no way that I can get 200 or 300 or 400 apps in a month when offices in the Dayton area weren't even getting 100 or 200 total." And he was asking each and every one of his employees to hit 100 or 200 or whatever the case may be.

At times, I thought our quota was overwhelming, but at the end of every month, we'd always be at that number.

With all these pressures, AL also wanted me to study for and pass my exam for a Life and Health license by September in preparation for my interview with Corporate.

I knew this test was of utmost importance, but I just couldn't find any additional time to study. I tried to study by myself without taking any courses to prepare for it. When I took the test, it wasn't horrible, but it wasn't good enough to pass.

One of AL's rules is that he will fund his team members for the costs of taking the tests, but you must pass the exams.

AL fired me. He believed that I didn't understand the importance of the opportunity he had given me.

I wasn't bitter. I knew he would fire me as soon as I saw my test results on the internet. I'd seen him fire a couple other people while I had worked there.

But I knew that I couldn't just stop there. I couldn't let that be the end for me. And I was very, very, very determined to prove to AL that I did know what an opportunity that was and that owning a business was the dream I've always had. Now I had to find a way to prove it to him.

A week after he fired me, I paid for the license exam fee and the books to go with it. I had to drive to Cincinnati where I took the test and passed it.

As soon as I passed it, I felt I needed to let AL know: (A) It had nothing to do with smarts. I knew I was always smart enough to pass the licensing test; and (B) It didn't have anything to do with the fact that I didn't appreciate the opportunity I had—I very much did. I just didn't give that test enough time on the very first go-round.

After I passed the test, I took it to AL's office, and I slammed it on his desk. I looked at him and said, "I told you I could do this. I knew I could do this. Here's the test. You can keep it. I just wanted to prove to you and to myself that I could do it."

I wasn't expecting anything, but AL immediately offered me my old job.

I don't think I even left the office. He told me to get started immediately. I went back to my desk—it was exactly the way I had left it—and I started making phone calls.

I ended up hitting 404 that month, and AL asked me why didn't I hit 405.

That's just the kind of man AL was with me, and then the next month, I hit 405.

He had just different mentalities and different ways of pushing me, driving me. It was unbelievable.

I just worked my tail off. I kept all my old weekend jobs. I'd stay at work until 8 or 9 at night. I kept that up until we got to Number One in the country.

I entered training for my own Agency in December when I pretty much dropped all the extra jobs. In June of 08, I opened up my own Agency.

And once you're done. Once you look at it when it's all said and done, you just kind of look back and say, "Man, he was good!" You didn't know what was going on at the time, but he knew exactly what he was doing with me that entire time.

I was intrigued by the fact that, if I was successful enough, I could own my own business. I was just absolutely intrigued by it. And the better we did, as the months went on and the closer we got to being Number One in the country, the more intrigued I got.

At each step of that year, I worked harder and harder because we were getting closer and closer. So I never really thought, "Aw, this is crazy." Or "This can't happen." I thought: "Wow! We're doing it!" And "We're gonna do it!"

As time went on, when that September-October-November time hit that year, and we were in the top two and three in the country, and we were biting at the heels of the Number One, it was just—I never thought that this man was in over his head. I thought: "Holy Hell. He was right."

I was like a pit bull chasing a steak on a stick. And my steak was the idea of owning my own business. I knew that if I could stand up to the challenges that he put in front of me, I hoped that if I could do that, his promise to me was that he would get me to where I am today. And it all came to fruition.

I think that the fact that he had that promise to me, that he could at least get me that interview—he can't sit in the interview with me, but he can get me an interview for my own business—having that there, I think that was the only motivation that I needed.

If you can promise me that—and he promised in the time span of a couple years—which he held right to. For two years, I was willing to break my back and work through blood, sweat and tears to get whatever he needed. Because at the end of that road, I knew what was coming to me.

I hope that one day I can return the favor to both AL and my Company for all they have given me. I am forever thankful and humble.

Anh Nguyen

Anh Nguyen never worked in AL's office. She started working in the insurance business nearly full time while she studied management at George Mason University. By the time she met AL at one of his speaking engagements, she had graduated and was an approved candidate working as an "additional intern" as she waited for an opening in one of her Company's agencies.

AL immediately offered to mentor her, and they exchanged many phone calls—every two or three weeks—between January 2009 and August 2009 when she opened her Agency in Alexandria, Va. They've stayed connected since then as Anh has adopted and adapted many of AL's systems into her business that has three full-time and two part-time team members.

AL opened my eyes to the possibility of how agents could run their own business and be very successful from the beginning. I had seen the opportunity in this business, just because of the way it had been explained to me. I had seen that, if I'm getting a book of business, I can generate the income. If I can write a lot of business, I can make a lot of money. So that was my mentality.

Seeing how AL's team members were so motivated really motivated me. It kind of changed my business model. He just opened my eyes, to a point I had not imagined, about what the potential of this business could be.

It was a great experience being able to reach out to an agent like AL, a successful agent who is willing to talk to me. This also gave me the courage to reach out to other people as well.

In hiring my team, I just tried to give higher expectations up front. I made them clearly aware that I was not looking for "average." I wanted highly motivated individuals to work for me. I assigned them some tasks to perform and some books to read just to see how committed they'd be.

I hired people who are competitive because I want them to want to win, to want to be on top.

One of the first things that caught my attention during AL's presentation was his emphasis on placing high expectations, up front, on his team. I placed the high expectations up front, and my team continues to expect that we must do well because there are no other options. We always say that we do not want to be average, and that's what drives us to want to be on top.

One of the things I took from AL is to hire people at a low base and then give them incentives to grow. They like that idea of having the opportunity to grow as persons. I encourage them to want to be agents. AL influenced me in a lot of different ways such as just teaching the staff to be more competitive. It's not really teaching them, but as AL would say, "Creating an environment for friendly competition."

The most powerful thing I learned from AL was teaching everyone to pivot. That's how most of our sales are made. I trained my team how to pivot. When people call in, it's not just a service. When they're calling in on the phone, insurance is on their minds. You need to maximize that opportunity. It definitely works. Pivoting is the key.

Within two weeks of opening the office, I showed AL's video "Perfect Day" to my team. They were like, "Oh my God!" And so I asked them the question, "How is AL able to do it, and why can't we?"

When we were in our third month in the business, we had the highest Life production for a new agency in the Maryland–D.C.–Virginia area. We had 72 applications and the next one down was 65. So that was exciting for them.

Another thing I learned was to have specialists in the office. I have a Life specialist, an Auto specialist and a Fire specialist, and they concentrate on marketing in those areas. They are the ones who I come to with questions in their areas of expertise. And they teach each other.

At team meetings we discuss successes and failures so that we can learn and so we don't make the same mistakes again. That idea is from AL.

I'm not the most organized person. I'm a people person. One of the things AL taught me is to get people to fill in your weak spots. AL's system actually helped me to be more organized. Having systems in place actually helps.

Another thing I learned is AL's desk system and how we make the work flow. My team members are trained to put notes in the system. They keep their files in a certain order. This way, if they are not here, we will be able to find the file and help the client.

AL also recommended separating Sales from Service so things that take sales more time to do are given to someone else. I actually have someone who fills out applications so that my salespersons can concentrate more on bringing in the sales.

When I'm away, at planning conferences and things like that, I meet other Agents who are always checking in at their offices and really scared that their team is not doing what they're supposed to. I don't have that worry because I have confidence in the people I hired and their income is dependent on how much they sell. So I know they're not slacking.

AL has the production board idea with all the colors. So we have a large production board in back. We have a creative guy here, and *he changed it up a little. He made cars with magnets. We have fun with that: "Look how many cars I have! Look how many Fire policies I have!" That idea is from AL, and we adapted it to our office.*

I also use color, as AL suggests. In our office, I have bright colors on the walls, and everybody talks about it. Our office has fuchsia, lime green and red.

AL really taught me to think outside of the box, to think big and to set high goals and expectations and to use systems so everyone does things the same way every day so that we continue to improve and to grow progressively more efficient every day. With all that in place, we could do our own "Perfect Day."

Devan DeClue

In the Fall of 2009, Devan DeClue, a 24-year-old office manager who spent 13 months with the AL Sicard Agency, was wrapping up her duties in Dayton as she prepared to move to Irvine, Calif., and a salaried position as an Agency Intern in an Agency near her Company's training office.

She is at the step before becoming an Agency-owner. After about seven months of additional training in California, she will work with other local agents until an Agency opens up for her there.

Meanwhile, her vision board was being framed by her father.

"I thought it was kind of crazy, at first," Devan recalled of her first instructions from AL. He directed her to construct a replica of her most wonderful dreams—it turned out that some of her dreams were actually those of her parents.

On it, she had pasted pictures of palm trees, symbolizing her goal to live in California. There was a Mercedes Benz, a nod to her mother's "dream car." The Los Angeles Lakers team logo found a prominent spot on the board, too. Her Dad's favorite team had become hers. And she wears a Lakers ball cap to work.

Devan found a picture that said "Number One Agent" in our Company and clipped it out. And finally, there is a photograph of a huge tiffany ring, in anticipation of a marriage yet to come some day in her bright future.

Devan had been a junior at The Ohio State University, working as a part-time, event planner and cocktail waitress at a local restaurant often frequented by AL and his wife. Recognizing her exceptional energy and enthusiasm, AL arranged an internship with a competing company's Agency after she graduated with a dual degree in business and international studies. When AL had an opening in his Agency in Dayton, she moved there.

"I always wanted to own my own business," she said.

Devan was assigned the color "green."

"I didn't really care about the color," she said. "I probably would have liked purple because of the Lakers."

At AL's Agency, Devan did not just develop skills running an agency and selling insurance. A quiet, young woman, she had always shied away from public speaking.

"I would shake. My hands would get clammy," she recalled. "I told AL, I would not speak."

AL took that as a challenge. He took her with him to a speaking engagement he had in Missouri. She had barely been at the Agency a week, and she was ordered to prepare a speech for 30 people she had never met.

"I drove my team members crazy," Devan said. "Everyday, I was practicing. When agents came to visit, I would speak in front of them."

When she walked into the room in Missouri, there were 200 business executives waiting.

"AL thought it was funny," Devan said. "I had some trouble with the microphone. I was a little distracted, but I got through it. It wasn't bad."

Greg Orton

Greg Orton graduated from Purdue University in 2009 where he was a standout wide receiver on the football team for four years while studying for a degree in Organizational Leadership and Supervision in the university's College of Technology. The Cincinnati Bengals signed him as a free agent and then waived him before the season began in 2009.

At the time of the publication of this book, Greg was focused on three goals: working out for another attempt to gain a position on an NFL team; studying calculus and statistics on line to complete his degree at Purdue; and studying to take his Series 6 examination in preparation to sell mutual funds and variable annuities, one of the last steps to becoming an Agent-owner of his own insurance business. Ideally, Greg would like to play in the NFL while he runs his own Agency.

Greg's father works for a contractor at the local Air Force Base near Dayton and his mother works in banking. Their son has been working at AL's agency off and on since he was a high school freshman. Greg credits AL with encouraging him to read, to study hard and to open his eyes to a career as an insurance Agent, even if he becomes an NFL player. When Greg was 19, he got licenses to sell property and casualty and also for life and health.

Most remarkable of all, Greg found his own voice working at AL's Agency, making cold calls after school to overcome his extreme shyness. It led to a stellar academic record at Purdue, carrying a 3.8 grade point average his junior year, and his selection as one of three members of his team to participate in a three-day, major media event held in Chicago for Big Ten football players.

I first met AL when I was in 7th or 8th grade at Spinning Hills Junior High, and I was kind of struggling in school, kind of taking sports first. One of my favorite teachers, Miss Fisher, she was a science teacher, and she came up to me and said, "I know somebody who went through the same thing that you are going through."

At the time, I was like, "Okay. That's cool."

So, she kind of sets it up that we meet, and AL comes to the school.

The first thing I see is like, this red Corvette, and AL in this suit. And I'm like, "What does he do?" He was like an NBA player.

It was pretty crazy. I was like in awe when I first saw him.

We just talked. He had played basketball at the same school that I was at. At the time, basketball was my favorite sport. And we were kind of from the same neighborhood, which was cool. And he was telling me what he does, that he owns his own business and works for this insurance company.

From that moment on, I knew, that after sports was done, I wanted to do what he does.

AL and Greg sat down and talked. AL still held the scoring record in basketball at the junior high school Greg attended. AL gave him *The Magic of Thinking Big*, the first of many books that Greg, not a bookworm then, would delve into. When Greg entered Wayne High School, a school with a highly regarded football team and receiving coach, he also began working part-time for AL after each football season ended.

That was my first job. I loved it. Just talking with AL, and seeing him. It was like being with Michael Jordan and being able to practice with him.

It was definitely an eye opener. And the reason he had me read those books is that I had a problem just talking to people—just being open and talking to people. He told me to study good speakers. I did that. I would watch my pastor talk. I would watch people on TV talk and kind of just get a little bit from everybody.

After football season ended, twice a week after school, Greg would drop in at AL's Agency where Greg spent an hour or so making cold calls.

He had me making calls and working with the full-time people, but mainly it was just to job-shadow him so I could see how his business works.

On the phone, I would just tell them, "Who do you have?" and "What are you paying?" Then I would tell them, "We have this, and we could offer you another thing with a multi-line discount."

It would be rare that I would talk to many people. It would be after school, around threeish, and a lot of people were at work, so I would get a lot of answering machines. At the time, that was kind of good, because I was kind of nervous about talking to people. But I got over it. The more people I talked to, the more I wanted to talk to.

It actually helped me out. When I got to Purdue, and I got more of a name for myself, they would ask me to go talk to schools and talk to the YMCA and spend time with those people. And there was no fear in me about it.

At the time, I didn't think too much about it. But now, looking back over it, you know, I kind of think of those skills and those facts that I learned and I'll just apply them to my Agency one day.

It wasn't much money, but now I really see how he was working with me. I really had to be self-conscious about a lot of things and just learn a lot and take good notes, which was really good.

He took me under his wing, and he taught me certain things that I took to Purdue with me, and that I took to the Bengals. Just about networking and reading books and increasing my knowledge in certain areas.

During summers away from Purdue, Greg studied and passed licensing exams so he could sell to the customers he previously had only tried to contact as part of AL's telemarketing team.

We would do mock interviews to learn to talk in front of people. It really helped me with my media interviews when I got to college. And it helped with the Big Ten Media Day. My school selected me to go to it where I could talk about my team.

By the time I got to college, I mean, I was comfortable. I like talking to people. I like to get to know people and really, just network with a lot of people. I like to just sit back and learn from people.

In the aftermath of his bid for a position on the Bengals, Greg continues to elevate his "B" game at AL's Agency.

He's taught me everything I need to know. He's got me watching different movies and reading even more books. So, it's getting even more crazy. Definitely, I've learned a lot from him. And he showed me that the most important thing, the biggest thing I can do, is to always keep giving back to my community.

I feel like this is something I was just born to do. I've been doing it for almost ten years. I have all this knowledge. I worked for him. I've always been in his office—constantly talking to him.

This is always something I wanted to do, and now I'm really excited that the time is finally coming for me to do it—and to still do my dream with football, too.

Ben Raymond

Ben Raymond was an observer-intern at AL's Agency for about three months during 2007. After that stint, Ben entered an Agency training program in Texas.

In August 2008, Ben opened an Agency in Irving, Texas. Using AL's systems, Ben already is assisting two persons trained at his Agency into "scratch" agencies of their own in Atlanta and Houston. He has fully embraced AL's systems, with two full-time team members and one part-timer along with a number of high school interns who work half days for credits under a program with the local high school.

Ben played basketball at the University of Minnesota, Duluth. His wife, Tamika, a professional basketball player and assistant women's basketball coach at Kansas University, played for the same high school as AL, and she worked for AL during several summers while she was at the University of Connecticut.

I've always been passionate about sports. Obviously, I didn't make professional basketball—that was my obvious dream—but my other dream was to always run my own business. Tamika worked for AL some summers while she was in Dayton. Later, we were living in Columbus, Ohio, and Tamika, who knew I wanted to own my own business, said, "AL wants to talk to you."

I said, "Who's this AL guy?"

I didn't really necessarily believe it at first. A lot of our alumni from Minnesota went on to work in insurance in different companies and in different roles. They were running offices and not being their own bosses. So, I was a little bit turned off by that, at first.

Yet, I agreed to sit down with AL. We had some more conversations. He showed me one of his paychecks, and I looked at it and said, "What is this? About three months pay?"

"It's the last two weeks' paycheck," he said. I just about dropped out of the chair.

"You've got my attention, loud and clear."

First, AL had me read a lot of books: Magic of Thinking Big; Power Position Your Agency.

He had me thinking and getting into the correct mind-set.

Then, step-by-step, he showed me the systems that must be put in place. AL and I are 100 percent alike. We're very competitive; we have athletic backgrounds. So I kind of understood where he was coming from. I was on his wavelength about why I needed these systems. I just couldn't understand how it could be this easy.

How could it be this simple? But I trusted our relationship and accepted that everything he was saying was true. And it has been true.

He developed that culture and system so well, that when you start following that, you see that your team will go above and beyond the call of duty. And that's what I'm starting to see now.

If they don't want to be Agents, we don't want them in our office. That's their motivation. The training that they're getting before they open their own Agency's doors should be the motivation to work hard. We should never have a work ethic situation in our office.

I have one team member who is really passionate about becoming an Agent. This person has taken the financial sacrifice now.

Insurance is tough. But if you were to ask someone: "Come in for a one, two or even two-and-a-half year period. Work hard and you're likely to earn $100,000 a year for the rest of your life, not to mention being backed by a top-30 company in the world. Would that be of interest to you?"

When you position things like that, people really, really pay attention.

If someone really wants to be their own boss and take those risks, it's a certain characteristic, and you usually can weed that out pretty quickly.

Right now, when I'm interviewing a high school or college student for a position, I have team members telling me that "so-and-so" is not going to be a fit. So my team is dictating who is going to come in here because they are starting to understand the culture and the meaning behind the attitude and the work ethic. They realize they can't allow people in the office who will slow them down and hinder them from getting what they ultimately want.

I've put two into Agency. One is opening up in Atlanta, Ga. The other is opening in Houston, Texas. Both are opening up new agencies. One was sent to me on a recommendation. The other was in another industry. One worked for me and the other came in under similar circumstances to the way I observed at AL's Agency.

The team member who worked for me came in for less than six months. I got him approved in my office, trained in my office, and got him into Agency from my office. The other one, who observed, read the books and sort of interned, also spent about six months in my office.

Their departures for Agencies have really fired my team up. I have one team member who wants to leave in a year and another who wants to leave in a year-and-a-half.

My biggest dream—well, yes, I want to make the money, and, yes, I want to own my own business. But my biggest passion in everything I've always done, whether it's been at camps in the sporting industry or elsewhere, I've always wanted to help people.

To see my team members grow and develop is why I do this everyday. To see somebody else carry the tradition and the legacy is my whole goal. I want to see people be successful.

I've never worked in a position my entire life where I never wanted to be away from it. This is something that I love everyday. There's not always going to be those great days, but I know why I chose to do this.

Travis Trice

A graduate of Butler University in Indianapolis, where he played basketball, Travis Trice ran a small business with his wife, and then he worked four years as a laborer in construction before he undertook a whirlwind trip through his Company's Agent-training program en route to his own Agency.

A month after AL first suggested that Travis consider a career in the insurance business, the Company had evaluated Travis and had him in a training program. Travis opened his own Agency in Dayton, Ohio, in May 2004, just seven months after he entered training. Today he has two full-time team members, one of whom has been with him since he started.

During his training, Travis was also pursuing a second goal of coaching a high school basketball team, while with his wife, Julie, raising four children. In 2008, they had a fifth child, their second daughter. Travis became a high school basketball head coach in 2007 where he coaches his eldest son, a junior already sought by Division I schools.

The beauty of being an Agent is that you are the CEO. You get an opportunity to work your schedule and to get the staff that you want and that you need.

You can make whatever kind of money you want. It's just a matter of owning your plan and working your plan.

It's been great for me. If I need to leave early, I leave early. I can come in early to get some work done. I can stay late. It gives you the freedom, not only financial freedom, but the freedom to control your time a little bit.

Travis hasn't missed an event that involved any of his kids.

Right now, all four of my older kids are playing basketball at different levels. My wife and I have always wanted five kids. We've been together 19 years. I'm 37 and my wife's 35. We always wanted a big family. There's no sense in having a big family, if we can't enjoy them.

If my kids are interested in something, whether it's sports or theater, I want to be able to support them. This job has really given me that opportunity.

AL has been my mentor, and he's given me some great advice over the years. But it's more about not recreating the wheel. You have to go out and see some of the Agents who have been successful.

I didn't know anything about insurance when I started. I didn't know what my own insurance liability limits meant when AL first asked me about going into the insurance business. In my first training class, everybody in my class of about seven or eight had some type of background in insurance.

It wasn't so much about insurance. Insurance is the same everyday. This is about how you talk to people, and how you get them to connect with you in a short amount of time. You must build relationships with them so they will appreciate recommendations that you to give them about the right amount of liability for the style of life that they lead. They must see you as a professional who will help them to protect their family.

I became a professional in a short amount of time. I learned the products, and my Company has a great training program to help me learn the products. But the biggest thing for me was gaining an understanding of families and making families feel comfortable that I was going to do the best thing for them.

All I've tried to do is to take bits and pieces from Agents who are trying to get it done, who already understand what they are trying to achieve, and adding that to my office.

When I got into this business, I already had the competitive background, and my Company appreciated that in 2003 when I applied to be an Agent. I had to work and scrap and claw for everything that I've achieved, and a lot of that grew out of my competitiveness as an athlete. I played basketball at Purdue for a couple of seasons before I moved to Butler where I continued to play.

The biggest mistake I see some of the new Agents make is they just throw money out all over the place. They throw money at the wall and see what sticks. That's a comment I hear a lot.

You have to be smart about what you are spending your money on. The key to not getting into trouble at the start of owning your own business is to not put yourself so far in debt that it becomes a frustrating hole that you are trying to dig yourself out of.

When I first got my Agency, it was in Dayton, and I was living in Springfield. It wasn't too far, but I wanted to get my face out there in Dayton and to spend some money doing some things in the community.

If you are doing things at sporting events or at the Rotary, that's free advertising. I think you need to get as much out of free advertising as you possibly can. The easiest way is to get out and get involved with the kids or to get involved with the senior citizens of your community. Make sure they recognize and know who you are. That really, really saves you money in the beginning.

In Springfield, before I got my Agency, I was already coaching Little League sports. Parents there knew, if I was as good as I was with their kids, they knew they could feel comfortable with me handling their insurance.

When you are entering a community where people don't know you, I think it's even more important to get out and get involved in areas that aren't the easiest to do. Anytime you see kids or people in the community are signing up for things, simple things, like a registration for basketball or football or baseball, it's important to come out and have your sign and your picture out there and to be there to hand out some cards and brochures, things like that.

It doesn't have to be sports-related. It can be business meetings in town. You may have a service that an attorney in town can use or you can recommend an attorney. It's about building those relationships.

If you've got the personality to gain relationships in a quick manner, then this is a great business.

Cynthia Brown

Cynthia Brown, a C.P.A., worked in public accounting and private industry before she turned to the insurance business.

Surprisingly, the process moved so quickly that Cynthia did not have an opportunity to spend six months working in AL's Agency as planned. Instead, she had to drop in a week or two at a time to try to pick up the skills she needed.

Cynthia owns an Agency in Maryland, just outside of Washington, D.C. where she grew up. She also serves as Board President of a non-profit performing arts company. They develop artistic productions and conduct art-based community outreach in both Washington, D.C. and New York City. She is a dancer, choreographer and student of theatre performing techniques.

She began her Agency training in April 2006 and opened her Agency the following December. She has two full-time and three part-time team members. Two of them aspire to be Agents in the near future.

Cynthia's Agency connects to the community through youth-related avenues. At the local high school, she recruits and sets up booths at P.T.A. meetings and sporting events. At the elementary schools, she teaches classes, speaks at career day and attends book fairs. She also supports local little league teams. As a result, many of the children's parents, teachers and school administrators have become her clients.

AL convinced me to give insurance a try.

I worked in a high stress, high performance environment. So when you are making six figures and someone talks to you about becoming an insurance agent, you might ask "Why would I want to do that?"

If I had it to do all over again, I would have started right out of school!

I was very successful in my prior career, but I felt that there was still something that I wanted to do—something more connected with helping people where I could have a sense of fulfillment in what I do everyday. It's great to have a nice paycheck, but it is even better to earn money and make a difference in other people's lives. I also wanted to see what it was like being an entrepreneur.

So, I took a risk and agreed to do it.

Wow, was it a different environment!

My training process was intense. I relocated from another city and lived out of a suitcase for six months while preparing for Agency. I recommend for people coming from an industry other than insurance, to really take the time and spend at least six months in a high-powered Agency environment like AL's. It may feel like a sacrifice, and you may take a huge salary cut initially, but you learn to execute systems so that you can train, coach and motivate your own team. You will understand products and feel confident interacting with clients. It also helps you visualize how you want your own Agency to run. If I could do it all over again, I would have slowed down and done exactly what I mentioned. I am certain that it would have made my transition smoother.

I started Agency with a team member who had a lot of insurance experience because I felt that I needed someone who understood the business. Being new to the industry, it made me comfortable at the start, and it was extremely valuable. All of my systems, however, were met with opposition, and after about six months, I realized that I did not have the energetic Agency environment that I wanted. I had to retrain and transform my team member's thinking or hire people who were open to both growing the business and retaining clients.

I needed coaching on how to fire. The first time was the worst. AL told me that if I have to ask "Should I?" or talk to three other people about it, I already know the answer. Just do it and do it fast! Well, I witnessed that attitudes, both good and bad, spread quickly. I finally did it, but not fast enough. AL was right.

Before I opened my office, AL told me to recruit constantly. I agree that the team is our biggest investment and our biggest asset. Recruiting is an essential part of Agency forever.

Like most Agents, I spent time looking for a "salesperson" when I really needed a person with a positive attitude and a willingness to learn. AL told me to scout for people who took pride in delivering great service—from your doctor's office, to the bank, to your favorite coffee shop. It is my job to train and coach.

Determining starting salaries for team members was the next challenge. I completely disagreed with AL on how easy it is to find talented people with college experience at the salary he recommended. Maybe it was possible in Ohio, but certainly not in Maryland. But sure enough I found her. Then I found another. They made my Agency and my life so much better.

She was like a breath of fresh air. She was very eager and interested in the Agency opportunity. I took the same training program that AL talked about relentlessly. First she started as an intern, and now she is full time and moving in the right direction. She was exactly what I wanted and everything AL told me that I could find.

Insurance experience is not as important as a positive attitude. Actually, insurance is not difficult. It is easy to understand once you *make it simple—breaking all of the information down into "Baby Terms," as AL says. This works with training the team and trickles down to our clients.*

I had a customer in my office just last week, and I was explaining life insurance to him the same way that I always do. He said to me, "You know, I've bought three life insurance policies for my family, and I've never understood them until now." He felt as if he knew enough to go out and teach somebody else. My experience has been that customers who understand and feel empowered naturally refer their friends.

A great training tool I adopted was videotaping. My first team member was very knowledgeable, but when I suggested the videotaping concept, she refused. That was a sign. I explained that I was uncomfortable my first time being taped too because I was not prepared. It never happened again. I rehearsed in front of the mirror, with family, friends and anyone who would listen.

When my new team members started taping, I could see immediate results. They told me that it heightened their awareness of the fine details, and it allowed them to practice until it flowed. I think the confidence helped elevate them as insurance professionals.

When I started, I thought I needed to have my hands on everything in the office. I was a team member, not the CEO. When I took time to train my team and trusted my team, I was more focused. So, another learning curve for me was how to completely remove myself from the business. The faster your business runs without you, the better your life will be. I'm not saying stop working. I mean work on the business and add to it what you do best.

My background was financial related, so I naturally gravitated toward the parts of the business where I was most comfortable. For me, that was meeting with clients about retirement planning, financial services, and investing. I didn't spend as much time on property and casualty, so I developed a system for everything. I also coordinated my marketing around my systems.

Some of the systems are related to sales and others are purely operational. The "once and done" is one of my favorite operational systems. In a day, we might have hundreds of phone calls, emails and requests. So we don't have time to handle something twice. We try to close the request the first time, but it is not always possible. We pick a date in the future to follow up, and then move on to the next item. All of my desks are the same inside and on top. There is a place for every piece of paper.

We use scoreboards to help motivate the team and to coach. A lot of Agents only choose to measure lag indicators such as how many applications were written during the month. Well, when the month is over, how do you know what needs to be adjusted to improve the next month?

If you also measure the lead indicators, like the activities that drive results, you'll see where you need to increase efforts. You will be ready to answer the following questions everyday:

- *How many appointments were set?*
- *How many quotes were given?*
- *How many referrals were received?*

I hope that sharing my challenges will help someone else. The Agency opportunity really changed my life. It opened my eyes to a whole new world where I could make money and be rewarded in so many different ways.

Deseral Neal

Deseral Neal's first job at the age of 19 was working as a mail and file clerk in the New Jersey regional office of a major insurance company. During the next 18 years, she had two children and went through a divorce as she took jobs in every department of the Company's regional office, including recruiting new Agents, while she attended William Patterson University (B.A. Aug. 2004) and Kean University (M.B.A. in business management, Jan. 2008).

She entered Agency training in January 2008 and opened up her Agency in December 2008 in Plainfield, N.J., using only the funds allocated from the Company's start-up allowance.

Deseral has three full-time and two part-time team members, all of whom started when the office opened. She just started a paid internship program for a single-mother student from a local high school.

Every different position that I've had, I've taken something from it. And with my schooling, I've brought it all together.

I was an Agent-recruiter for a couple of years, so I knew exactly what it took to be an Agent.

I also worked in marketplace compliance. I went to Agents' offices to make sure everything the Agents were doing complied with the Company's guidelines. And I worked in Auto Claims, so I had dealt with customers on losses and everything of that nature. I could explain later, as an Agent to my customers, what will happen and what role I will play when a claim is made.

Of all the things that I credit my success to, first and foremost is that I had a strong support system. I have a very tight-knit family who live in New Jersey. I have two sisters, and my Mom and my Dad are now both retired. They helped me with the kids, and also gave me emotional support.

I married right out of high school. I had my son at 19 and my daughter at 21. As a single mom, I didn't have a boatload of money. I really didn't have a fallback if this didn't work, or if my first couple months were bad, I didn't have additional money to cover it.

So I was very cautious when I started.

First, every new Agent must understand that it doesn't start when you open your doors. It starts way before then.

When I first found out where my location would be, I came to Plainfield every single day of the week, and I drove around to find the areas that were the most congested. Once I found that area with the most congestion, I knew where my location would be. And I began to look for an office that had everything I would need. I did not have any build-out expenses.

Next, I met with the Mayor and told her of my plans to open a new Agency in town. She introduced me to the other council members. Plainfield is an urban area, and I was bringing revenue to their town. They had a lot of resources, and they gave me a grant that paid for all of my signage.

Before my doors opened, everyone knew who I was. The Chamber of Commerce had a big ceremony for the opening of my office. This was all free marketing that I didn't have to spend anything for. All the local newspapers came to the opening, and the Mayor was there to cut the ribbon.

And all of this was what I created because of everything I had done earlier.

I hire differently than most Agents. I don't ask the normal questions when I hire. I want to know your background, and I want to know where you are coming from, what's going on in your life, where you are heading and that you have a plan to get there.

I know, in my career, I was overlooked for a lot of positions I had put in for, just because maybe I didn't have that degree at the time or because I was a single mom, they didn't think I could handle it.

But I know what type of worker I am, and from my past experiences, what made me that type of person.

I have three full-time team members, including a 22-year-old, former real estate agent who wanted to switch careers when the housing market collapsed, a 27-year-old divorced mother of two young children and a 45-year-old, recently divorced father of three kids. I have a part-time bookkeeper who runs all of my systems and works full time for the local schools. I also have a part-time college student who performs clerical work and contacts customers to obtain information or documents we may need. Neither part-timer works in sales.

I looked for aggressive people, and I gave them a low base salary. I pretty much told them that they would have to make their money based on what they sold. It made them money, and it made me money to keep me going.

I did not spend a lot of money on marketing. I only sent out mailers. But because of everything I had done before I opened, when my doors opened, my office was packed, and it stayed packed. It's all walk-ins and referrals.

If I'm not here, the office runs without me.

I do a lot of community service. I do health fairs for the local churches. I do defensive driving courses for the high schools.

Plainfield High School has a nursery at the school for all of the teenage parents who attend. Every single mother at the school is eligible to compete for a paid internship in my office. They are evaluated on a point system that considers their academic achievements and their participation in three different training seminars that cover resumes, job applications and interviews. If they have a job, they can get out of school at one o'clock.

I'm also hosting a Christmas party for all of the babies in the High School nursery. All of this touches my heart so dear. Sometimes, with the right mentor, all they need is a little push, and they'll be fine. They'll excel to unimaginable heights.

Deseral appreciates the distinction between entrepreneurship and intrapreneurship.

Intrapreneaurship is when you own your own business, but under a Company that already has established it's brand. Intrapreneaurship is what you do under that brand.

It's a kind of freedom to have your own business, but it comes with a safety net because you're not creating anything. You know the brand of your Company is successful. It's what are you going to bring to make your own Agency successful.

For me, that's what I was looking for because, as a single mom, I needed that safety net and support system.

Blending the safety net of the Company's brand with the emotional support of her family became an key objective for Deseral.

I say, make your children a part of it.

My children have been a part of me and my Company forever. When I had my homework, we would gather at the kitchen table. I would be doing my homework; they would do their homework. Kids mimic what you do.

When my son graduated from eighth grade, I graduated from college. When my daughter graduated from eighth grade, I graduated from graduate school.

My son is a freshman in college now. He's a straight-A student. My daughter also is an honor roll student.

After we had our grand opening, and the Mayor and everyone came to my Agency, my son rode home with me that night.

He said, "Mom, I am just so proud of you, and I hope that one day, I'll be just like you."

Speedy

During my first year of Agency, my father was stricken with cancer. The news just buckled my knees, and as I drove to the hospital, I was thinking, "Oh, my God, what's going on?"

Dad had never been ill. When I arrived, I was told he had pancreatic cancer. It wasn't good news at all.

I went to see him in his room. Dad is a military guy, a very, very smart engineer in the Air Force. He served as my first accountant for my Agency. But he refused to let me see him.

"He doesn't want to see you unless you have 100 apps on the front run ," I was told, understanding that I had to show him I made 100 sales.

I went back to the office, faxed the reports to show him we were doing well, and I then I got to see my Dad.

He loved me to death, and I returned it all as best I could. And then, it seemed like in the blink of an eye, he passed away while I was still in my first year.

I was shattered. I turned my attention to my mother. I actually obsessed about trying to help her, trying to fill my Dad's shoes while remaining a grateful son in her eyes.

Shortly after my Dad's death, I won a trip to the Bayou Classic football game. It's a classic southern rivalry between the same two teams each year, Southern University and Grambling State. They play before capacity crowds at the Superdome in New Orleans. My first Bayou Classic was an amazing event because I took my mother with me.

When we arrived in New Orleans, I quickly realized that this thing was nice. My mother was starstruck. "Whooo-oo," she was saying. "My son made it!"

I arranged for one of those shiny limos to drive us around the city. This was before the hurricane, and the driver's talking about everything in the area as we drive past.

The prize included a stay at the Ritz-Carlton on Canal Street. As we got out of the limo, I was trying to think of little things I could do to make this a spectacular time for my Mom.

"Can you get some chocolate covered strawberries?" I asked one of the hotel attendants. "Yeah," he answered.

"Can you get the white chocolate?" "Yeah, we'll mix it together and everything. As a matter of fact, we'll check your bag and take it up to the room for you."

I was so impressed; so was my mother.

Since we didn't have to go through a long wait to check in, I quickly began looking around to find something to entertain my mother. That's when I saw these horses and buggies. "Let's go over here," I said.

This elderly man approached us, and in that special Louisiana drawl, you know how it sounds, he said to me, "A businessman needs to see his face in his shoes," And he knelt down and began polishing my shoes!

I got the point—immediately. I asked if he could take my mother and me around the downtown in his carriage. It was like I had offered him a small fortune.

"Great!" he said. "What's your name? Where are you from?"

He began telling stories and asking more questions. My Mom's just laughing and just beaming with pleasure. It felt great. It was great.

As the horse and carriage pulled away from the curb, the driver leaned back and said, "My horse's name is Speedy."

I was taken aback. This horse had gray hair, its nose was almost touching the ground, and its back drooped between its neck and tail like a slack hammock.

Now, I'm a big guy. I was a power forward in NCAA Division I basketball. And I began wondering, Can this horse pull me?

But the driver didn't seem to be concerned. He was just talking away, and Mom's smile got sweeter and sweeter.

"This is where I grew up," the driver said, engaging us with his own personal history. "Emeril Lagasse used to be a kid on the playground, and I used to beat him up all the time. This is where I met my wife. This is where we kissed the first time. This is where we proposed."

This is really cool. I was enthralled, and I could see that my mother's eyes were moist, probably from a mixture of pleasure and relief. I could see this had begun the healing process for her after losing my Dad.

We came around a corner, and suddenly the driver snapped, "Come on, Speedy. Come on! We gotta win."

I'm thinking. Man, we—we barely made it this far with that horse.

But Speedy is going now. Speedy is making this a race. I could see that his legs were still slow and heavy and probably tired, but his head was up like he was winning.

I'm thinking: "Speedy is blind."

It was a great event. My mother thought it was a great event. And I tipped this guy a ton of money—$70. Well, that's what they call a Trainee Agent's tip. For me at that time, $70 was a lot of money.

In fact, in those days, I had to check the balance on my credit card just to check into a hotel like the Ritz.

* * *

The next year, I didn't win a return trip to the Bayou Classic, but I decided to take my grandmother to it anyway.

My grandmother is Jamaican and a little British. She's snobby. Actually, she doesn't like anything, except her kids and grandkids. But I was determined to show her a good time.

"This is a great event," I promised her.

Since I hadn't won anything, my plan was to try to recreate that feeling that had so captivated my Mom and me a year earlier. But it was just me and Grandma going to the Bayou Classic.

Here's how it went:

We got off the plane, and I have a limo for her—not the same, shiny limo that we had taken the first year, but it's a passable limousine. The limo driver did a good job, but it was different, maybe not quite as pleasurable as the previous year.

Before we got downtown, the first thing my grandmother noticed was that there was dust in the limo.

Then we drive past the Ritz, and my grandmother says "Here's the Ritz. What's going on?"

"Grandma. This is on me. We're not staying at the Ritz. We're staying down here at the Sheraton," I told her. She's mad now.

"Your mother stayed at the Ritz, and now we have to …"

"Okay. Whatever."

So, I get out of the limo, and I'm asking attendants at the hotel, "Can I get some chocolate and . . ."

"Naw. We ain't doing any of that. You need to go to registration to see if you can even get in," they told me.

So we stayed some time in the hotel lobby, checking in and then carrying bags to our room. It took about 15 or 20 minutes.

My grandmother was getting tired, but I was determined to give my grandmother an equivalent experience to my Mom's.

"But you ought to go on this horse and buggy ride," I pleaded.

She relented, and we headed out the hotel door. But we ended up at the back of a long line that I thought was a line for all of the horse carriages.

"I'm not waiting in no lines!" Grandma announced.

My Grandma was acting up in front of everybody. I frantically searched for another horse and carriage. There was one with no line!

"Come on, Grandma. Just get on this one horse," I said, with a confident tone in my voice that I was hoping would not betray my increasing sense of distress.

And we get on the carriage. This guy runs us around the block, but he didn't say one word to Grandma. There was no connection. No aura of wellbeing. No sense of family or friendship. No sharing of little bits of personal experiences. Nothing.

Now, who do you think that line was for?

Speedy.

The two horse and buggies do the same thing. Just like any two insurance Agents.

In my town, there's a guy down the street whose Agency writes 50 applications a month. My Agency writes 300.

We do the same thing. Or do we?

Do you think Speedy and his driver create that same experience shared by my Mom and me every time he steps away from that curb?

People keep coming back to him.

Summary

I cannot overemphasize how important it is to understand that you are running a business and not just an insurance Agency.

In other words, you are hiring people who are looking up to you for advice—not just about Agency—but about their own careers.

If you only care about them for production, then you will create a ton of problems within your Agency. These problems can be overlooked in the short run, but never in the long run.

Here's my test: Consider that one of your team members is out on the weekend and is asked, What do you do for a living? If that team member's answer includes only your Company's name and doesn't mention the name of your Agency, then you have a problem.

In this book, I've tried to explain that doing the work up front will make an easier transition later on. Putting together the systems, the hiring process, the procedures manual and the handbook, will result in fewer problems for you later on.

With this advance planning, you will just have to run the systems, rather than let the systems run you.

In creating an Agency that works without you, you stay out of the New Agent Graveyard, you create a better family environment and you appreciate how great this business can be.

When I'm on trips with the best Agents in the country, I can see how they have adopted these systems. I also see that these top Agents earn triple the earnings of most Agents while they work less than most Agents' typical 60-to-80-hour workweeks.

Most Agents believe you can motivate team members just by giving them bonuses. I believe you can motivate team members by recognizing them and by creating a career path for them.

It makes no sense to me to think that the only way to motivate team members is through bonuses. We forget how great it feels to be recognized, even though we love to be recognized, to be praised, to be talked about and to be featured in books and magazines. But we conclude, mistakenly, that no one else would want that type of recognition. We forget how great is the yearning to have a career in which you will be taken care of for the rest of your life.

We're in a career we love and that we know will take care of us. Why can't we do the same for our team members?

I think the reason is that most Agents don't like the jobs they are hiring for. They feel these jobs are sales jobs—door-to-door and cold calling. If you don't like the job, how can you tell your story to the new hire?

If you take away one thing from this book, you will realize how important it is to use part-time people to take away some of that drudgery from the full-time team members. Let your full-time team members enjoy working for you while they passionately pursue a career in this business.

BigAlf.com

This web site published by AL Sicard offers books, DVDs, training programs and a weekly, drop-in demonstration to assist Agents and their team members in grasping the finer points of *Creating a Business That Works Without You.*

AL keeps an updated schedule of events at locations around the globe. These stimulating events offer new and experienced Agents and their team members up-to-date training in AL's numerous Systems.

AL also offers a blog from the website. From here you can find links to AL's Facebook, MySpace, Twitter and RSS.

Why BigAlf.com? That's what the big guy has been known as since he gave up being small.

About the Author

A 1989 McDonald's All-American and varsity basketball player for the University of Dayton in his hometown, former power forward AL Sicard has taken the art of owning a small business—insurance businesses, in particular—to a new level.

A widely-sought public speaker, AL is regarded as an authority on explaining corporate culture and developing best practices for insurance companies.

AL's spectacular performance for his Company and his commitment to the annual Read & Rise program, an annual scholastic event for youths co-sponsored by the National Urban League, have garnered the attention of top celebrities, including Oprah Winfrey, who is his mentor.

In supporting an annual fund-raising event attended by thousands who support the study program, AL brought to Dayton speakers such as Oprah, poet and actress/director Dr. Maya Angelou and Wall Street banker Raymond McGuire. For his community activities, AL was named 2006 Man of the Year by his hometown.

As a trainee agent with just three, full-time team members, AL captured his Company's "Fast Start Record" by submitting 367 applications for auto insurance in three months. More recently, AL elevated his team's performance using a promotional concept he calls "Perfect Day." In a single day, his team produced 102 insurance applications.

In 2007, AL's small agency in Dayton surpassed all others in his Company for writing fire insurance applications. Recognizing AL's outstanding achievements, his Company made him an Exotic Traveler, a member of the Company's Advisory Council, and a qualifier to the Chairman's Circle and President's Club.

In 2006, AL was featured in a remarkable State Farm "True Story" commercial broadcast during Super Bowl XLI.

At State Farm since 1997, AL rose from Agency Specialist at the Company's Newark Operations Center to Specialist in the Dayton AFO. He chose the agency career track and became a trainee agent in July 2000.

AL has worked for other international companies. He was a marketing manager for General Motors Leasing Division, selected by its Minority Dealer Owner Program. He also owned and operated an auto leasing company.

AL has been an invited speaker before audiences at international corporations such as Yahoo!, Proctor & Gamble Co., The Coca-Cola Co., The Walt Disney Co., The Allstate Corporation and Nationwide Mutual Insurance Co.